Divine Intimacy
Your Journey to Purity and Holiness

Linda Chiyoge

DEDICATION

This book is dedicated to Jesus Christ. Father, I thank You for trusting me
with this vision, thank You for providing provision to complete this
assignment. Everything that I have belongs to You. I am absolutely lost and
empty without You. This entire book is dedicated to You and I will
continue to be obedient in every task and commend that You present
before me. This is a kingdom tool that will bless and impact many
generations to come. Daddy, this is a gift that You have blessed me with
but I give it all back to You just like Hannah, you gave her a precious gift, a
son and she gave him back to You. I give this book back to You!

TABLE OF CONTENTS

ACKNOWLEDGEMENTS

First and foremost, I'd like to give my Lord and Savior Jesus Christ all the glory and honor for the inspiration, divine strength, and wisdom to write this book. It was not an easy journey but with perseverance and prayer He made it possible. Thank You, Jesus.

I'd like to acknowledge my parents who have always loved me unconditionally. To my prayerful mother, Nsimire, for always demonstrating the love of Christ, patience, and so much grace: thank you, Mommy. To my father for always being there for me and loving me. I'm always going to be "daddy's girl." You are the best father a daughter could EVER have! I mean that from the bottom of my heart.
I love you both tremendously.

To spiritual father, Dr. Bishop Kibby Otoo. Thank you for your endless prayers, selfless disposition, and genuine love. When I was broken and lost, you held my hand and raged war for me in the spirit! You brought out the best of me even when I didn't know who I was! I am spiritually equipped today due to your mentorship and guidance. You are my daddy and shepherd! Thank you for teaching me how to slay demons and destroy the work of darkness. I thank God that, because of you, I'm a prayer WARRIOR! I love you.

To my siblings, Nyota and Jean Claude, I am forever grateful for your compassion towards me. Thank you for always standing by my side and supporting me. You embraced me during the most difficult season of my life and I am forever full with gratitude towards you. I love you.

To my other siblings Eric, Iragi, Aganze: thank you for always loving me and believing in me! The three of you will never lose your place in my heart! NEVER.
I love you.

To my godparents, Aimee and Ernest. I thank you for standing by my side when I hit the lowest point of my life in 2009! You fought for me spiritually and never gave up on me. I am forever grateful. I love you.

PROLOGUE

My journey to celibacy wasn't easy...

I know that most of you that have been following (I) @Jck_Brand on social media are wondering, "How did this all get started?" And "How in the world has she gone 6 whole years without penis?" I understand why you would be curious so I want to keep it real with you! Prior to embarking on this journey of celibacy, I was just like you, having sex with my (back then) boyfriend on a regular basis and still attending church. I prayed daily, spoke in tongues, and honey.... I would tear up a dance praise...break into a sweat, shouts and all. I attended service Wednesday night, Friday night and Sunday morning.

I faithfully served in the house of The Lord and yet I still struggled with lust. There were times that I would cry and repent repeatedly about the sexual acts I was committing. I would ask for The Lord to forgive me. Yet I would fall right back into the same trap days later. I had to admit to myself that I was addicted to having sex with my boyfriend. It seemed unfathomable to me at the time to not have sex with him. It was so much fun, it felt SO good, and was a major release for me. Inside I also struggled with worry and thoughts that if I didn't sexually please him that he would leave me for another woman. I know that most of you ladies today are experiencing the same struggles and fears, and I understand. But I want you to know you're worth more than hot sex, fancy hotel rooms, and sexual fantasies. You are worth SO much more than any of that!

You see, I had established a soul tie with my boyfriend and this was why it was so hard to let go of him. Our spirits had become intertwined and our souls were connected and bound; due to fornication. Based upon biblical precepts, we had become one spiritually. This is why you have to understand that sex is not just a physical act, it goes much deeper than that. It is far beyond our emotions and just a 30-60-minute sexual act! I know I gave you a lot to think about.

What's your reason for fornicating?

One of the reasons why you're still fornicating is because you have "worldly and carnal" ways to justify satisfying your flesh.

You **know** it is wrong, but you continue to engage in sexual acts. This was me too.

I had all kinds of reasons to justify having sex outside of marriage:
We love each other.

We are going to get married someday.

If I don't give it to him, he'll cheat on me... (Girl, he was cheating on me anyway!)

He was so good looking I couldn't resist.

I don't see anything wrong with it.

Everyone else is doing it.

We didn't go all the way.

All those reasons listed above are fake and lies from the pit of hell. The devil will always deceive you and have you seeking to glorify your flesh...he makes the bad look so good it fools you into believing it's truth.

Porn and masturbation also nearly destroyed my destiny. After I made a vow to Christ that I would refrain from fornication, one of the things I continued to struggle with was porn and masturbation. Yep, I would do it in my car, in the restroom at work, at home or wherever it felt safe and I knew no one   was watching. I missed having sex with my ex! I was still tied up and in bondage, lusting after him! Many nights, I would dream that he and I were having sex. This was all due to the soul tie I had established with him. Other times, a creature would violate me sexually in my dreams and I   would try to escape, but couldn't.

You may say "Oh Linda, it's just a dream." But NO, IT IS NOT, trust me! I am sure that these dreams happen to most of you! It's all driven by the incubus spirit which operates through a sexual demon, which you opened yourself to through sex, porn, and masturbation. It gains total ground and control of you from these three activities.

The enemy wanted to keep me in sexual bondage and tried to destroy my destiny and calling. Can you imagine? Had I not been set free from this, I would not be here today helping hundreds, and soon thousands, of women become delivered from this stronghold. The enemy wanted to completely keep me in the dark so I could not be a light to others. But he failed.

Here I am today, almost 6 years free, and helping other women gain back control over their bodies and destinies. I am so blessed and thankful to be where I am today! I don't ever have to worry about my emotions being a wreck, creating soul ties with a man that is not yet my husband, and catching STD's. It is a blessing. I am exactly where God is calling me to be and that is where I want you to be too.

Sometimes you gotta laugh at your pain...

Lord have mercy! Now when I look back on my life, sometimes I just laugh and **praise God** for my deliverance. I struggled with insecurity issues because my boyfriend constantly cheated on me and I would always run back to him because I wasn't strong enough to be on my own. I thought the best way to keep a man was through sex and pleasing him. I would go over and above to please him sexually. I did all the tricks!

From Missionary to Doggy Style, oral sex, whatever he wanted. I would act out all of his sexual fantasies; in his house while his mother and sisters were home, in the car in public parking garages, hotel rooms...you name it... been there done it all!

But my soul was still empty and unsatisfied! All I was doing was satisfying my flesh and his physical needs. God was not in this mess. The

Holy Spirit was **far** from us. This relationship was dark, it was dishonoring to The Lord and it sure was not healthy for me at all. Our relationship was based on sex, although we loved each other – or I can say I THINK we loved each other. It boiled down to how good I was in bed and how far I would go in terms of pleasing him. Well, my friends, that cycle came to an end. I now know better because I fought VERY hard to get to where I am today.

But now, unlike me, you don't have to do this alone! The Lord placed it on my heart to create The Divine Intimacy book to help you escape. To teach you how I did it and what I did, to overcome all of this, you are definitely in for a treat in with this book.

It's time to put your foot down!

You have a tough soul decision to make! The truth of the matter is you're going to have to make up your mind and put your foot down once and for all or continue to be lost in the world. This decision is going to be difficult. It will cause you to lose a few people in your life… Like your boyfriend whom with you fornicate or sex partners… Also, your freaky girlfriends that talk about sex 24-7 and encourage you to indulge in it as well.

When you decide to be different and set yourself apart from the crowd, you will need to literally be separated from people and from the distractions in order to focus on God. In making this commitment, He will deliver you and set you free. Leaving my ex was hard. I thought we had something so special. I really thought what we had was love and I lied to myself thinking it would eventually lead to marriage. And it did not. Don't be fooled by your emotions. **FYI:** the writing is typically on the wall.

So maybe you're also at a place of fear, scared of losing the same person that is pulling you away from God. You're afraid to lose those very people that cause you to sin and fall short of the Glory of God. You are afraid you'll never find anyone else like them. **Girl, please!** The Devil is a liar and so is his mother-in-law! HA!

YOU deserve to be with someone who respects you enough to wait until marriage to dive in and explore your goodies. Let me just tell you that the blessings of God don't come in a form of sin. They are not manipulative and they don't make you feel guilty! Think about it! In **HIS** blessings you are free. In **HIS** blessings you are fruitful. In **HIS** blessing you glow: there is glory! In **HIS** blessings, there is no fear.

God's love is pure and free for all those that seek him with their heart!

THE DAMAGING EFFECTS OF SEXUAL IMMORALITY AND PERVERSION

Peradventure, you are on the verge of committing a sexual sin; be it fornication, adultery, or masturbation. In that wise, you will find this content quite helpful as a wake-up call. Though it might come to you hard, and somewhat damaging, to the belief systems you have developed over time. Just hold on, your deliverance should be your utmost aim.

At times, things that are meant to be good may be dangerous if abused or misused. When you dig deep into the context around which such things are done, you would realize the danger thereof, and therefore gain the insight you need to stay clear of them. As the saying goes, not all that glitters is gold.

God created sex and it's a powerful means to intimacy for married couples. In this case, sex is good. But then, sex, when taken out of the right godly context, can be dangerous and deadly to one's spirit. Sex comes in a variety of ways—legitimate and illegitimate.

Fornication Defined

Fornication could be defined as an illicit sexual activity between opposite sexes outside of marriage. In high schools, colleges, and universities, many of our youths are actively involved in such sexual abnormality, but seemingly normal and acceptable to them. Unfortunately, the entertainment industry has worsened the situation, as the average youth practice of what they see on movies and TV shows. It's no wonder why most don't see the detriment in sex outside of marriage. People continue to date and have sex with strangers with little or no sense of moral remorse. Fornication is now generally considered normal in our society and people continue to justify their ungodly acts. Some people feel it's meant to prove love for each other. Others worry that their partner would not remain interested if they do not partake in the act. All of this is untrue. What then would you say about sex-dating between strangers?

In addition, fornication is not limited to sex. One can be guilty of fornication when someone or something else takes the place of God in one's life. Take for instance; a number of times, God accused the children of Israel of "whoredom" or fornication, when they served other gods, idols, or when they loved things above Him.

So, when a thing has become an idol in your heart because you have an inordinate desire for it, you are guilty of "whoredom." It goes as deep to the fact that even if you don't physically commit the act but consciously imagine or think about it, you are as guilty as when you act it out. On that note, in Matthew 5:28, Jesus says, "I say to you that everyone who looks at a woman with lust for her has already committed adultery with her in his heart."

Other Forms of Sexual Perversion

- **Incest:** takes place between two relations; e.g. a father who sleeps with her daughter has committed incest.
- **Adultery:** sex between a married person and someone else who may be single or married.
- **Masturbation:** the stimulation of oneself for sexual pleasure; its habit forming.
- **Pornography:** watching nude people have sex; for example, in porn movies; it sexually arouses the person and contaminates the mind.

All of these can cause the formation of a soul tie. Here is the first truth you must embrace:

Whether you commit "whoredom" by acts or in thoughts, you will face the same damaging effects that such a sin could bring upon the soul.

Dangers of Fornication

"I know Ephraim, and Israel is not hidden from me; for now, O Ephraim, you have committed fornication, Israel has defiled itself. Their deeds will not allow them to return to their God. For a spirit of fornication is within them, and they do not know the Lord" **(Hosea 5:3-4).**

Now, let's consider the evil that comes with fornication so you can know how serious the issue is before God.

1. **It brings defilement to your being—soul and body. Song of Solomon 2:15** says, *"Take us the little foxes that spoil our vine."* To be defiled is to be spoiled, perverted, corrupted, damaged, destroyed, polluted, or ruined. Such a sin will cause a loss your dignity and the sanctity of marriage will be destroyed. The soul becomes impure and sick. When God says to keep yourself pure, He means well for you—it is for the good of your spiritual, mental, and physical health.

2. **It brings separation from God.** The given Bible text tells us that such deeds will cut you off from access to God, no matter how religious you may be. You may even be in church, and God is talking through His minister, but your guilty conscience won't let you get closer to God. Your confidence before God will be gone and as a result, you will want to avoid places or words that prick your heart in the area of your sinfulness. It's no wonder why most of our young ones are outside church falling deeper and deeper into fornication to the extent that they no longer see anything immorality in the act. In their heart, they don't want to go to God. Remember, Adam did the same thing when he sinned in the Garden. Guilt makes some people run far from God. But that's not the solution to their problem.

3. **It permits an unclean spirit to indwell you.** The devil, through his demons, is waiting for chances to invade and possess the body of anyone that engages in sexual sins. Demons gain legal ground to enter people who commit fornication. In the case of Ephraim and Israelites, the demon is named the spirit of fornication. Why do

such spirits seek to enter people? They want their victim to be entangled in fornication, and that's why it's VERY hard for some people to break free, even after they have repented. That little seemingly harmless romance and sex has turned into passion or habit.

Before you know it, the victim will be moving from one sexual partner to the other. In some terrible cases, the person will be sexually insatiable, as the demon will give him/her an excessive libido. Moreover, the evil spirit may lead the person into other harmful areas such as lies and falsehood.

4. **It brings weakness and sickness to the body.** Today, the most common ailments are STDs and HIV/AIDS.

5. **It causes ungodly soul ties between the lovers.** We'll go into detail about that later.

6. **It brings eternal damnation.** *"Knowing the Lord is eternal life; but those who reject His statutes will be condemned to hell."* **(John 17:3)** This point alone is enough for every fornicator to repent. Keeping this in mind, no one should trivialize the issue of fornication as though it has no grave, no grievous consequences on both the body and the soul. It's never pleasing to God as it steals one's heart from Him. The victim of fornication repents and calls upon the Lord for forgiveness along with deliverance. Without this, he or she cannot live well; be it spiritually, mentally, or physically. Don't be deceived; the sin might appear to be fun, but always bear in mind that there are repercussions when committing it.

Soul Tie Defined

The term soul tie is a concept often used to describe a deep, soul-realm bonding that takes place between two people in a relationship that involves sex, friendship, covenant, or oath. Although we may not find the term in the Bible, there are events that attest to its reality.

The idea was suggested in the friendship between David and Jonathan. The Bible says the soul of Jonathan knitted with that of David. The concept however originated in the Garden when the Bible says that when a man cleaves to his wife, both shall become one flesh. The Apostle Paul also mentions that when he rebukes the Corinthian Church it would be absurd to join harlot to the body of Christ. All these instances talk about soul ties. It's something very difficult to break.

Side Effects of a Soul Tie

In simple terms, we could state that it's a phenomenon whereby two souls bind together in the spiritual realm. For a married couple, they become one flesh that cannot be put asunder. For fornicators, a soul tie is damaging. Earlier on, we said that an evil spirit can enter a fornicator and make the person always desire sex; even assuming an evil spirit is not there. This soul tie explains why some people find it hard to break free from abusive relationships. Imagine a lady who cleaves to a macho, sadistic guy; even though she dislikes him, she still comes back.

Obviously, some soul ties have the ability to wreck the soul. Have you ever heard of a situation where someone would run into an ex and glue to him/her at first sight? Imagine a married woman who receives a call from an old high school boyfriend, only to connect with the person and find herself engulfed in a full blown affair. It implies that soul ties can manipulate you against your wish. Sometimes you might not even be aware that you're under an ungodly control. If you have had multiple sexual partners or divorced and remarried a number of times, you may find it difficult to bond to your new partner.

Soul ties can facilitate the transference of evil spirits and demonic elements from one person to the other. If you've had sex with someone whose life has been infiltrated by evil spirits, you would be open yourself to the same demonic influence. Soul ties bind you to curses and/or problems your partner has experienced. Christians who fall into the sin of fornication are open to demonic filth in the life of the other person.

Causes of Soul Ties

Here, we would like to look into some of the ways by which soul ties develop between two people who engage in fornication:

1. **Sexual Acts:** As said earlier, sex can be legitimate or illegitimate based on the standards of Scripture. In the same vein, soul ties could be either godly or ungodly.

   Godly Soul Tie: This is developed between married couple. *"For this cause shall a man leave his father and mother, and shall be joined unto his wife, and they two shall be one flesh"* **(Genesis 2:24)**. This is a God-sanctioned, unbreakable bonding between a husband and his wife. That's why divorce is not an option in turbulent marriages. Though our society and man-made marriage regulations permit that, *"God hates divorce"* **(Mark 10:7-9)**. Wait a minute. We're not talking about people who cohabit here; such individuals are living in fornication—they are not legitimately married in a holy matrimony.

   Ungodly Soul Tie: This is developed when two unmarried people have sex, when a single person has sex with a married man/woman, when someone is raped, and when relatives commit incest. *"What? Know ye not that he which is joined to a harlot is one body? For two, saith he, shall be one flesh"* **(1 Corinthians 6:16)**.

2. **Intimate Friendship:** We made reference to the friendship of Jonathan and David; both souls knitted together in a good friendship. *"And it came to pass, when he had made an end of speaking unto Saul that the soul of Jonathan was knit with the soul of David, and Jonathan loved him as his own soul"* **(1 Samuel 18:1)**. We could easily deduce as well that a negative or evil soul tie can develop in bad relationships. Have you heard of young ones that went the extra mile to commit a crime because of what they saw on their favorite TV or listened to in their music?

3. **Words:** The Bible warns us to be careful of what we say since we shall either be justified or condemned by our utterances. While dating or courting someone, you make promises to the person; you're bonding yourself to that person regardless of the fact that you haven't had sex. "You're my love forever," "I'll never love any other lady/guy like you," "We are together for life," "I've given you my heart," and such like things, flow from the mouths of human beings. *"Whoso keepeth his mouth and his tongue keepeth his soul from troubles"* **(Proverbs 21:23)**.

Our utterances, depending on the context, could be oaths, commitments, vows, or agreements. Sometimes we think or feel that what we say is just a promise when, in context (though unknown to us), it's an oath. All these bind the soul. In marriage, we make vows and that's acceptable. But in dating or courtship, if your words have gone out to a person you once dated, even if you didn't have sex together, you have probably formed a soul tie with him/her.

Steps to Breaking Soul Ties

1. **Repentance of the sin of fornication, if that is the cause in your case.** Don't excuse it. Sin is sin, and forgiveness only comes when you acknowledge it. Ask God to cleanse and justify you by the blood of the Lamb.

2. **Get rid of all items you received from your sex partner, no matter how precious the gifts might be.** Don't tell yourself, "Oh, what a precious diamond ring!" Exchanging of gifts serves as a seal to the bond, the soul tie. Those greeting cards, flowers, fashion products, love letters, photos, and others, throw them away in the bin.

3. **Cut your ties with your sex partner.** In other words, don't be close friends again. Stop visiting and calling. If the person is a member of your church, limit your contact to church; don't go to their home. As for co-workers in your workplace, let them know their limits. All these will keep you from falling into temptation.

4. **Renounce every word of promise, oath, agreement, and vow that you have made to the person.** Verbally renounce those so-called statements of love you have spoken under the pressure of your crush or lust for someone's body. Break the oath with another Bible- based statement in the name of Jesus. "In the name of Jesus, I renounce the word of oath, agreement, commitment and promise that I made to (name the person) when I told him/her that I'll never love anyone besides him/her…"

5. **Forgive the person and forgive yourself.** Maybe you have developed a bitter, resentful spirit toward the other person. You must let go to let God. Complete healing starts with receiving forgiveness from God when you let go of those hurtful feelings you have for one another. Forgive! Again, forgive yourself for walking

into the arms of a strange person whom God didn't intend for you as a partner. "For Christ's sake, I forgive so-and-so for..."

6. **Renounce all soul ties.** "In the name of Jesus, I renounce all ungodly soul ties formed between (name the person) and myself when we had (name the sin) ..."

7. **Finally, break the soul ties.** Using the power of the name and the blood of Jesus, command the bond to break and release your soul. "In Jesus' name, I break the ungodly soul ties formed between (name the person) and myself because of our (name the sins) ..."

Demons of Fornication

In the previous section, we didn't talk about getting ourselves freed from evil spirits. In **Hosea 5:3-4**, we read about the spirit (demon) of fornication. So it's not enough to break the soul ties, it's essential you receive deliverance from those demons too. Before going into that, let's look at two other manifestations of this spirit.

1. **Incubus:** an evil spirit that sleeps with women while they are asleep; it's a sexual demon in masculine form.

2. **Succubus:** a sexual demon in the feminine form that comes to have sexual intercourse with men when asleep.

They are also referred to as "night demons" or "sex demons." Their job is to defile people. They are spirits of sexual immorality and perversion. The other manifestation is acting as the demon (spirit) of lust. The demon attacks people during sleep because in those hours, the person is unconscious and the body is in rest mode. Such that there is little or no control over what's happening around them. Most times, those attacked by an incubus or succubus spirit can feel penetration, but won't be able to wake up until the sexual act is over.

I also previously mentioned people having unusual libido as a result of demonic influence. The spirit of fornication can cause that. I've heard about people who claim that they can't do without having sex every day; sometimes twice in a day. This is abnormal. Another way to discern the work of this demon is when you are under the pressure of temptation to sin. Maybe while at work, home, or on an outing, your mind is being bombarded by lustful thoughts so strong that you seem unable to shake them off. You may be under the attack of sex demons. In such a situation, you would be overtaken by the thought that you can only find bodily release by engaging in the act, watching pornography, or stimulating yourself to orgasm. If the thoughts persist, you may eventually have the orgasm from the effect of sexual scenes formed in your imagination—this is usually called a sexual fantasy. Those demons flood your imagination with obscenity; if you feel you have no control over it, you will fall for the trick.

Nevertheless, it's worth noting that not every sexual urge you feel comes from demons. Sometimes, they may arise from hormonal changes in the body. For example, some women often feel a sexual urge immediately after their menstrual cycle resulting in a natural urge to physically connect with your husband. After all, any sexual activity between a married couple should be naturally preceded by a desire for the others' body expressed in a close, romantic, sexual connection. Whatever the case, you should be able to control it. That is, if the urge comes and you can silence its voice, you're in control. But if it comes and everything you do to stop it is not working, this may be a sign that this evil spirit is at work.

Spirits of fornication can make people have sex dreams wherein they are having sex with someone, or they are watching graphic sexual acts between two people in that dream. It usually comes with a spontaneous orgasm. At times, these demons take advantage of the activities we do in our waking hours to oppress us. Imagine what would happen to a person who watches porn, love stories, or looks at a woman lustfully.

Being under the influence of these demons is highly damaging to the overall well-being of an individual. It's not fun at all. It adversely affects the victims spiritually, mentally, and emotionally. That's why they must seek urgent deliverance.

For the believer, an incubus/succubus spirit tends to impregnate their host with fear, lukewarmness, lethargy, and complacency which will pervert your Christian life. For the unconverted, the demon worsens their state unto damnation. They impregnate people with lust to make them desire fleshly things. They are the mastermind behind sexual perversion of all types—they use the hosts to increase the sexual related pollution in today's world. When a demon host sleeps with a person, he shares the evil seed with the individual. Sexual sins then continue to be on the increase. Many of our teens today have had sex at least once and they are likely to have more because the spirit of fornication has been transferred to them.

From sexual sins, the person may become pregnant and then go for an abortion (which is murder.) He or she may start going to clubs and parties sleeping with strangers. With time, the person may fall into Satanism as he or she begins to experiment with a lot of fleshly things like smoking, alcoholism, horoscopes, etc. The primary aim of the demon is to take their host far from God to the point of damnation.

INTRODUCTION TO YOUR JOURNEY OF
DELIVERANCE

So you know I have been celibate for 6 years now and I will continue until I get married. I don't even desire sex anymore. Just the thought of sex outside of marriage makes me want to puke! I am so excited that you have decided to embark on this journey! I am very honored that you have become part of what The Lord birthed out of me. This book is truly something that the Lord placed in my heart and I had to obey. Pre-marital sex is a tool that the enemy uses to abort, to sabotage the destinies of God's children and you have been falling for it. Now is the time to defeat it!

Before we get started, there are few spiritual exercises and prerequisites you must practice in order for the next 21 days of this spiritual journey to be effective and serve its divine purpose.

Three days prior to setting out for the journey, you need to engage in fasting for a spiritual detox, the reason being that you must be free from all sorts of behavioral attitudes and spiritual filth that are displeasing to the Lord God. In view of God's standards of living, ungodly cultural, mental and spiritual influences, tendencies, disposition, and beliefs that you have grown up with over the years can adversely affect the effectiveness of this challenge. Of course, you are in the world but not of the world, and therefore, you can't keep yourself from having a physical contact with the world but you don't have to imbibe their culture to the detriment of your spiritual health. With this fasting, you will be able to detox your soul so you can enter the realm of spiritual purity God has in mind for you **(see 2 Corinthians 7:1)**.

During the fast, refrain from food from 6 am to 6 pm. You can drink water and consume smoothies only. Almost like the Daniel fast. Then at 6 pm when you break the fast, eat veggies, salads, greens, and fruits only. If you are able to consume water only from 6am to 6pm, great, that's even better! But please don't push it if you can't stick with the first option. If you do struggle with fasting or have never done so before, just do your best. You might have to break it before 6 pm, but it is possible for you to go all the way. You can also replace your regular meals with veggies, greens, fruit, and/or water.

Here is what you should focus on during the 3-day fast:

1. **You must disconnect from anything and everyone that leads you to fornicate.** Get rid of all the sex toys you may have. Destroy every pornography video you have stored on your devices. Delete all filthy websites from your phone and computer.

2. **Refrain from secular music that promotes sexual**

provocation—yes, those so-called love songs too—from the likes of R. Kelly to the most current artists that sing about sex with explicit content. In this day and age, majority of worldly artist only sing about illicit romance and sex! Get rid of that playlist from your gadgets. The temptation is too irresistible for you not to be led into sin.

3. **This next one may be the most difficult thing to do, but you have to discontinue communication with your current sex partner(s).** If he claims that he "loves you," he would respect you enough to wait until marriage and he should understand that sex is no longer an option in your relationship. If you have to cut him off completely for him to understand your virtue, then do it. You have to make a solid decision. It's either him or GOD.

4. **Do not listen to secular music at all.** This means in your car, at work and home. Change the station to a Gospel channel or insert your favorite gospel CD.

5. **Don't attend any events or gatherings that promote anything that displeases God.** This most certainly includes parties, nightclubs, etc.

6. **You will need to purchase communion wine (grape juice) and olive oil.** We will take communion every day of your 21-day journey and use anointing oil ten of those days.

Luke 22:19-20 says, *"And he took bread, gave thanks and broke it, and gave it to them, saying, "This is my body given for you; do this in remembrance of me." In the same way, after the supper he took the cup, saying, "This cup is the new covenant in my blood, which is poured out for you."* **Revelations 12:11** *"And they overcame him by the blood of the Lamb, and by the word of their testimony."*

Putting on hair extensions, getting your nails done, and buying shoes to look good is all great, but very sad when your soul is contaminated and polluted. If you have been fornicating, watching porn and masturbating, then it definitely is. It is so amazing how women love to look good physically, but their spirit is dying and their relationship with Christ is dry. Can you imagine what your soul looks like? Right now. This very moment.

SPIRITUAL DETOX BY FASTING
Why Fast? What Does It Mean?

The Bible tells us that fasting is abstaining from food, drink, sleep, or sex to focus on a period of spiritual growth. Specifically, we humbly deny something of the flesh (in this case sex) to glorify God, enhance our spirit, and go deeper in our prayer life. Although fasting in Scripture is almost always a fasting from food, there are other ways to fast. And again, in this case, you are refraining from sexual activities.

DAY 1 FAST

Today, I just want you to relax and take a deep breath. Clear your mind and thoughts from anything that may tend to distract you and cause you to go astray from this fast. If this includes minimizing your social media interactions or activities, please do so. If what it takes is to send those obnoxious phone calls to voicemail, please do. If what it takes is to block certain phone numbers, please do.

You need to set an atmosphere for the Holy Spirit to abide.

SCRIPTURE TO MEDITATE:

Set a timer on your phone that will alert you to meditate on the following scriptures below every 5 hours daily, starting today:

1. **1 Corinthians 6:18-19** *"Run from sexual sin! No other sin as clearly affects the body as this one does. For sexual immorality is a sin against your own body. Don't you realize that your body is the temple of the Holy Spirit, who lives in you and was given to you by God? You do not belong to yourself."*

2. **1 Thessalonians 4:3-4** *"God's will is for you to be holy, so stay away from all sexual sin. Then each of you will control his own body and live in holiness and honor."*

3. **1 Corinthians 5:9-11** *"Do not associate with people who indulge in sexual sin. But I'm not talking about unbelievers who indulge in sexual sin, or are greedy or cheat people, or worship idols. You would have to leave this world to avoid people like that. What I am voicing is that you are not to associate with anyone who claims to be a believer, yet indulges in sexual sin, greedy, worships false idols, abusive, a drunkard, or cheats people. Don't even eat with such people."*

WHAT TO CONSUME:

From 6 am to 6 pm, you will consume only water, healthy green smoothies, tea and any other healthy beverage. You may eat veggies, greens, and consume water at 6 pm when you break the fast. You can also replace all your daily meals with veggies, fruits, water, and/greens.

PRAYER IN THE MORNING:

When you wake up in the morning, before heading to work or beginning your morning routine, pray this out loud and each time after you have meditated on the three scriptures I mentioned above: *"Father, I thank You for this opportunity to give my body back to You because it belongs to You. I repent for being selfish, disobedient, and ignorant. Forgive me for not aligning myself with Your word as I have been so consumed with pleasing my flesh. Forgive me for not allowing my body to be the temple of the Holy Spirit. Father, give me the grace to complete this fast and the spiritual journey. I want to grow within You. I want to have the deepest intimate relationship with You Lord Jesus. Help me and guide me. Thank You for the strength and supernatural ability to resist the enemy and sexual temptation. In Jesus' name, Amen!"*

ASSIGNMENT:

Choose one of the three scriptures mentioned earlier, jot it down on a sticky notepad and stick it on your car's steering wheel, your desk at work, and everywhere that you will be able to see it often throughout the day.

EVENING:

Before you sleep tonight, spend 20 minutes in worship or quiet time with the Lord. Meditate on the same scriptures. At the end of this chapter, there's space for you to express your thoughts. Talk to the Lord and release anything that's in your heart regarding your journey so far.

DAY 2 FAST

You will repeat everything from yesterday because the Lord wants those same scriptures to really go deep and steer your spirit. I am just being obedient to His instructions. So, go back to Day 1 and repeat the entire module.

EVENING:

Before you sleep tonight, spend 20 minutes in worship or quiet time with the Lord. Meditate on the same scriptures. At the end of this chapter, there's space for you to express your thoughts. Talk to the Lord and release anything that's in your heart regarding your journey so far.

DAY 3 FAST

You will repeat everything from yesterday because the Lord wants those same scriptures to really go deep and steer your spirit. I am just being obedient to His instructions. So please go back to Day 1 and repeat the entire module.

EVENING:

Before you sleep tonight, spend 20 minutes in worship or quiet time with the Lord. Meditate on the same scriptures. On the next page express your thoughts. Talk to the Lord and releasing anything that's in your heart regarding your journey so far.

Congratulations, you have completed the 3-day fast! Tomorrow you will begin Day 1 of The 21-Day Celibacy journey! Glory to God. For the next 21 days, you will continue the fast from 6am to 6pm. If it is too difficult for you to go without food from 6 am to 6 pm for 21 days, you may eat veggies and fruits only during the day. You are about to embark on a journey that will change your life!

DAY 1: DEALING WITH THE ROOTS

Before you begin, remember, for the next 21 days of the journey, you are fasting...Wait, before you freak out and yell, "Ugh! Linda, Why?!" Relax, girl. It is a very simple fast. From 6 am to 6 pm, do your best to consume veggies and fruits only for breakfast, snack, and lunch. Also, you'll want to drink plenty of water. When you break your fast at 6 pm and eat a small portion of what you've been craving all day, you have to be careful not to overdo it. That means, don't eat a whole bucket of KFC Chicken just because you have been craving it all day. Eat with moderation. I'm sure this made you laugh. You also have the option to replace all your daily meals with fruits, veggies, water, and/or greens.

MORNING:

Good morning! So, here we are! I told you, I will make this as practical and as applicable as possible. This is the very reason why the content in this book is very simple digest. Let's move forward.

Before you begin your day today, you will meditate on the scripture mentioned earlier all day (every 5 hours). Set an alarm on your phone as a reminder, if you must! Remember, I told you to purchase grape juice to be used as communion? You are now going to put it to use and since today is the first time that you are using it, say this prayer before you drink it: *"Father, in the name of the Lord Jesus, I speak to this grape juice with authority and I commend it to lose its natural characteristics and to supernaturally obtain the Spirit of God, and to act as the blood of the Lamb on Your behalf. In Jesus' name, Amen."*

SCRIPTURE:

Meditate this word every 5 hours all day today. Set up an alarm on your phone as a reminder. Don't forget to mediate at work as well.

1 Corinthians 6:9 *"Or do you not know that the unrighteous will not inherit the kingdom of God? Do not be deceived; neither fornicators, nor idolaters, nor adulterers, nor effeminate, nor homosexuals."*

I love the word of God because it is undeniable, true, and firm. You cannot argue against it and this is why I am utilizing scriptures to back up my content in this book. So, with **1 Corinthians 6:9**, I will ask you one simple question, if Christ were to come today or if you were to die right this moment, would you inherit the Kingdom of God? Fornication is not the only sin that will take you to hell, but it is definitely one of them. Since this is what the book is all about, I am remaining on this subject.

Before any complicated matter is to be resolved, we have to deal with its roots and foundation. What you are dealing with is a sexual spirit. A stronghold that has to be broken. And we have to cast it out and uproot it. This will be our focus for Week 1 of the 21 days—dealing with the roots.

EVENING:

Your simple assignment before you sleep tonight is to pray and at the end of the day, you are going to write down the names of all the men you have slept with, including those who perhaps raped or violated you sexually. You will use these names in the prayer below.

In **Luke 22:20**, Jesus tells us that the cup is *the "new covenant in My blood"* and the Apostle Paul tells us that the blood of Jesus brings forgiveness of sins **(Colossians 1:14, Ephesians 1:7)**.

Proverbs 18:31" *The tongue has the power of life and death, and those who love it will eat its fruit."*

PRAYER:

Pray this out loud three times with power and authority. Don't say it under your breath. Get up and declare it loudly!

"Father God in the name of Jesus, I humbly come before You and thank You for Your mercies that are renewed every morning, including today. I ask You for divine strength to make it through. I rebuke every distraction and spiritual bombardment that the enemy has planned in order to interfere with this journey. Now, by the power of the Holy Spirit, I (say Your name), destroy every sexual soul tie between me and (SAY THE NAMES OF THOSE MEN). Father, by the fire of the Holy Spirit, let the soul ties be broken in the name of Jesus. I disconnect my soul and my mind from them, Lord God. I reject and rebuke the spirit of lust that developed from fornicating with these men. Father, purify my mind, my body, and spirit in the mighty name of Jesus.

Lord, I release Your fire to destroy and consume every sexual residue that still resides in my spirit due to fornication with these men. Father, let Your blood cleanse and renew my spirit. Amen."

Right before you go to sleep tonight, take a nice warm shower. When you are done, worship the Lord. Go to YouTube and in the search bar type "Hallelujah - Michael W. Smith with Lyrics." Let his song play as you spend intimate time with the Lord.

Remember you are still disconnected from those that cause you to fall short of his glory, those friends that promote sexual behaviors, those family and friends that engage you in filthy conversations. And, of course, you need to be completely disconnected from the one with whom you have been fornicating. Remember, temptation can make you fall again. If this man truly respects you and loves you enough, he will honor the fact that you are engaging in a 21-day spiritual journey to please Christ. The Lord will always come first, before him.

CONFESSION TO CHRIST:

On the next blank page, write at least 3-5 sentences describing the consequences of fornication in your own words. Start with: *"Father God, I now understand why fornication is damaging to my spirit…"*

This completes Day 1.

CONFESSIONS TO JESUS:

DAY 2: WHY YOU WANT TO BE DELIVERED

MORNING:

Good morning, Overcomer! The birds are chirping! I hope you had a nice rest. Glory to God, you are here to see another day! Today will be very simple and I won't bombard you with so much. I don't want this to overwhelm you as I know you already have so much on your plate! Take your communion right now and before you do anything this morning, go to YouTube and in the search bar type "Kari Jobe and Cody Carnes - Holy Spirit Lyrics" Let this song play as you spend intimate time with The Lord.

Set the atmosphere and invite the Holy Spirit in your day. This entire playlist is amazing by the way. It can really take you high in the Spirit.

You are still dealing with soul ties and those with whom you have fornicated in the past. Your assignment today is very simple, yet very effective. Keep in mind, we wrestle not against flesh and blood **(Ephesians 6:12)**. So we are going to continue to make these declarations out loud!

PRAYER:

Take your communion before you start.

"Father in the name of Jesus Christ, forgive me for not resisting temptation. Father, forgive me for getting pleasure from this sin. I am so sorry God. Father, in the name of the Lord Jesus Christ, close those doorways and break all legal ground that demons and foul spirits are using to harm me. My body is the temple of the Holy Spirit. Every ungodly sexual soul tie that still resides in me, I command you to come out and never return in the name of JESUS! You unclean spirit of (list the names of the men), be destroyed in the name of Jesus! Lord, have full authority over my body, mind, soul and spirit. Enter my body as the consuming fire and destroy every unclean spirit that dwells within me! Sexual addiction, I reject you and bind you in the name of Jesus. Go back to the pit of hell where you belong! I belong to Christ and I will honor Him with my body. It belongs to HIM!"

SCRIPTURE:

Meditate this word every 5 hours all day today. Set up an alarm on your phone as a reminder. Don't forget to meditate at work as well.

Meditate the scripture below every 5 hours during the day. Set an alarm on your phone as a reminder.

Ephesians 6:11-12 *"Put on the whole armor of God that ye may be able to stand against the wiles of the devil. For we wrestle not against flesh and blood, but against principalities, against powers, against the rulers of the darkness of this world, against* *spiritual wickedness in high places."*

1 Corinthians 6:16-17 *"Did you know that he who unites himself with a prostitute is one with her in body? For it is said, the two will become one flesh. But whoever is united with the Lord is one with him in spirit."*

CONFESSION TO CHRIST:

On the next blank page, write a one-paragraph letter to Jesus. Let this be at least 8-10 sentences. Write to Him and *tell Him why you no longer want the spirit of fornication to rule over your life.* Tell Him why He should deliver you. This sounds so cliché, but it works. Prayer works! Speak to your Father. When you are done, go back to the prayer you declared this morning and repeat it again out loud tonight.

This ends Day 2. You will make it until the very end. Stay encouraged.

CONFESSIONS TO JESUS:

_____
_____
_____
_____
_____
_____
_____
_____
_____
_____
_____
_____
_____
_____
_____
_____
_____
_____
_____
_____
_____
_____
_____
_____
_____
_____
_____
_____
_____

DAY 3: FLESH UNDER SUBMISSION

MORNING:

Good morning. I am so proud of you because this is definitely not easy, but with your dedication and applying all the instructions in this book, you can do it. Remain consecrated and focused.

I want to share something with you today. When I made a vow 5 years ago to honor God with my body, the day after the vow, the enemy came so strong! The desire to have sex doubled! I was so hungry for sex. It felt that if I didn't have it, I would lose my mind! So, masturbation became the enemy's new strategy because I was determined to refrain from sex. So for 3 years after making my vow to Christ, I struggled with self-pleasure and I was given to sex toys, and sometimes pornography, this is also a stronghold. I continued to battle with this sexual spirit! At times, at night, after masturbation, I could feel "penetration" in my vagina during my sleep. I later came to the revelation that the incubus spirit gained grounds and access to me due to masturbation! It opened me up for him to enter and take control of my body and spirit.

An incubus spirit is a demon in male form who, according to mythological and legendary traditions, lies upon women in order to engage in sexual activity with them. Its female counterpart is a succubus.

Before you go to work this morning, apply the anointing oil in your inner thighs (just a tad bit). As you are applying and rubbing it on, declare this:

"In the name of Jesus, my body is the temple of The Holy Spirit. I will not go against God's word. I will not allow myself to fall into sexual immorality today. I (say your name) will not indulge in anything that I not pleasing to the sight of my Father. I rebuke every desire of masturbation, pornography and fornication. Leave my life now, in the name of Jesus. The word of the Lord says flee from fornication and therefore, I am being obedient to His word today and forever. I cast out every sexual imagination, thought and action in the name of Jesus. Today, I choose to walk in holiness and purity. Today, I choose to honor my savior Lord Jesus Christ, Amen."

SCRIPTURE:

Meditate the scripture below every 3 to 5 hours today. Make sure to set an alarm on your phone as a reminder.

Ephesians 6:12 *"For we do not wrestle against flesh and blood, but against the rulers, against the authorities, against the cosmic powers over this present darkness, against the spiritual forces of evil in the heavenly places."*

EVENING ASSIGNMENT:

Remember, I asked you to purchase communion juice? Well, in this case, anointing oil can be used too.

PRAYER:

"In the name of the Lord Jesus, Father, I declare that Your Spirit enter this oil/communion. Let it lose its natural tendencies. Father, let it become a supernatural weapon that will destroy the incubus spirit and the desire to fornicate and destroy—crucify—my own body. You demonic spirit of masturbation, I rebuke you in the name of Jesus Christ! I command you to leave my body, leave my house, and leave my life. Leave my soul and leave my spirit in the mighty name of Jesus Christ! YOU HAVE NO AUTHORITY OVER MY BODY! YOU DON'T BELONG HERE! IN THE NAME JESUS, I DECLARE THE FIRE OF THE HOLY SPIRIT TO CONSUME YOU COMPLETELY. IN THE NAME OF JESUS, I DESTROY YOUR STRONGHOLD AND CHARGE OVER MY LIFE!"

I want to back up this activity with **1 Corinthians 1:27:** *"But God chose the foolish things of the world to shame the wise; God chose the weak things of the world to shame the strong."*

What you are doing may seem foolish and cliché, but it is powerful in the realm of the spirit. Let not your intellect or worldly understanding deceive you! You're shaming the devil by doing these "silly" things.

After you have completed your assignment this evening, worship The Lord for 20 minutes. Go to YouTube and in the search bar type "I Won't Go Back by William McDowell Lyrics"

CONFESSION TO CHRIST:

On the next blank page, write down a list of 5 things that you love about Jesus as it relates to this journey. Start with: *"Daddy, Lord I love You because..."*

This completes Day 3.

CONFESSIONS TO JESUS:

DAY 4: BE BOLD TO DELIVER SOMEONE ELSE

Good morning overcomer! Pat yourself on the shoulder for pressing through! Today will be similar to yesterday. The reason why we are repeating this is because the Lord has placed it in my heart that it is a very strategic activity. It is going to set you free as you do it by faith and take it seriously, especially if you are struggling with masturbation. What God is telling you to do and be obedient? Just DO it! There are three assignments today. Again, two of them are the same as yesterday's. The third one is different so please be patient until the very end.

We are going to focus on the same scripture as yesterday.

MORNING:

Before you go to work this morning, apply the anointing oil in your inner thighs (just a tad bit). As you are applying or rubbing it on, declare this:

"In the name of Jesus, no sexual demon or spirit will violate my body in the name of Jesus. By the application of this supernatural element, I will have no desire to masturbate or fornicate in the name of Jesus. I rebuke every desire to fornicate or to masturbate. No sexual spirit will attach itself to my body. I hate sex outside of marriage. I rebuke you in the name of Jesus."

EVENING ASSIGNMENT:

This assignment is going to be challenging but will save someone that you care about. Think of two people that you truly love and you know are living in sexual sin. Reach out to them via text message tonight and encourage them to rebuild and intimate relationship with Christ. Tell them why you have decided to do so as well and encourage them to refrain from sexual immorality. Don't attack them. Do it with love. Use your words carefully. Start the text with: "Hey (their name), I just wanted to reach out to you because I really love you and care about you. There is something very important that I want to tell you…"

PRAYER:

"In the name of The Lord Jesus, Father, I ask that Your Spirit enter this oil/communion. Let it lose its natural tendencies. Father, let it become a supernatural weapon that will destroy the incubus spirit and the desire to fornicate and destroy— crucify—my own body. You demonic spirit of masturbation, I rebuke you in the name of Jesus Christ! I command you to leave my body, leave my house, and leave my life. Leave my soul and leave my spirit in the mighty name of Jesus Christ! YOU HAVE NO AUTHORITY OVER MY BODY! YOU DON'T BELONG HERE! IN THE NAME JESUS, I DECLARE THE FIRE OF THE HOLY SPIRIT TO CONSUME YOU COMPLETELY. IN THE NAME OF JESUS, I

DESTROY YOUR STRONGHOLD AND CHARGE OVER MY LIFE! IN JESUS' NAME, AMEN."

SCRIPTURE:

1 Corinthians 1:27 *"But God chose the foolish things of the world to shame the wise; God chose the weak things of the world to shame the strong."*

What you are doing may feel foolish and inconsequential, but it is powerful in the realm of the spirit. Let not your intellect or worldly understanding deceive you! You're shaming the devil by doing these "silly" things.

After you have completed your activity this evening, worship The Lord for 20 minutes. Go to YouTube and in the search bar type "I Won't Go Back by William McDowell Lyrics."

CONFESSION TO CHRIST:

On the next blank page, write at least 5 sentences describing your experience with this journey so far. Speak to your father! What are you still struggling with? What has improved? What do you want Him to help you with? Start with: *"Father God, I am weak and hopeless without You…"*

This completes Day 4.

CONFESSIONS TO JESUS:

_____
_____
_____
_____
_____
_____
_____
_____
_____
_____
_____
_____
_____
_____
_____
_____
_____
_____
_____
_____
_____
_____
_____
_____
_____
_____

DAY 5: THE ANOINTING THAT BREAKS THE YOKE

Good morning, Overcomer! So, we are approaching the weekend, the weather might be warm and pleasant depending on the current season and your location. You may still have ungodly friends and they will start to "hit you up" and invite you to places that you know you should not go. It's the weekend. Don't get distracted. You are on a journey to honor God. A journey that is taking you to a divine appointment. Don't let that cook- out or party that will give you only temporary pleasure, deceive you. Don't let that ungodly boyfriend or ex of yours distract you. I am not saying to completely isolate yourself from people or social activities, but if the activities are not pleasing in the sight of the Lord, you shouldn't entertain them! You shouldn't be there. Period.

Look how God is giving you this amazing opportunity to change for the better. Yes, it has only been 5 days but let me tell you, He is doing a new thing in your life! Don't be discouraged! With that said, read scripture below:

MORNING:

Take communion. Go on YouTube and in the search bar, type "You Have Won the Victory with Lyrics". As the song is playing, say this short prayer: "Father God in the name of Jesus, this oil is anointed by Your Spirit. This oil is delivering me from the spirit of masturbation, pornography, sexual thoughts and fornication. I am sex free right now in the name of Jesus. No sexual demon will harass me and no sexual dream will be my portion tonight. I rebuke you right now in the name of JESUS!

SCRIPTURE:

Meditate this word every 5 hours all day today. Set up an alarm on your phone as a reminder. Don't forget to mediate at work as well.

Zechariah 4:10 *"Do not despite small beginnings."*

Isaiah 43:29 *"See, I am doing a new thing! Now it springs up; do you not see it? I am making a way in the wilderness and streams in the wasteland."*

EVENING ASSIGNMENTS:

Remember the sheet of paper that contains a list of all the men you encountered sexually? You are now going to put it to use. It's Friday and most churches hold evening services. Go to church tonight with that sheet of paper and a seed offering in an envelope. If your church does not offer Friday night service, find a house of the Lord near you that does and go. When you arrive in His house, don't hold anything back! Don't worry about who is watching you and how people perceive you. If there is an altar call

68

during service, go and rededicate your life to Christ with a seed in your hand as a sacrifice—no matter the amount—and the sheet of paper with the names. If there isn't an altar call, after services, go to the altar, kneel down, rededicate your life to Christ, worship the Lord, and make a vow to Him with your seed! That vow is between God and you. I won't tell you what to say. Leave that sheet of paper and your seed in an envelope on the altar and go. After service, go home and do your evening routine.

Your next evening assignment is very important. Something will take place spiritually. The Anointing breaks the yoke.

Today, the maxim, "Anointing breaks the yoke" fills everywhere we go within the church circle —it's now a mantra for most people, and many ministers have turned it into a kind of trademark. They even see or teach the anointing as a phenomenon that is greater in magnitude than Holy Spirit baptism; and anointing is that heavenly power required to break all manner of bondage and fetters that keep Christians from having a successful life. You need this power to break free from sinful habits, sicknesses, oppression, afflictions, financial indebtedness, and every other vice that contradicts the promises of God for you. It's therefore assumed, in some quarters of theology and religion, that if you're struggling with sin, sickness or any other issue, you are not yet anointed. Such a stance is as divisive as the doctrine of tongues that some Pentecostals have misunderstood.

Before you sleep tonight, take a nice warm shower or bath and relax. After you're done, anoint your entire body with the anointing oil; don't miss your inner thighs. As you're doing this, declare:

"In the name of Jesus, I am set free and delivered from the incubus spirit, sexual demons in the night. You will NOT violate my body and spirit. I command you to stay in hell where you belong. By this anointing oil and by faith, I declare for the yoke of sexual sin to break! Right now by this oil I declare the desire to masturbate is destroyed. Now, by the power of the Holy Spirit, I (say Your name), destroy every sexual soul tie between me and (SAY THE NAMES OF THOSE MEN AGAIN). Father, by the fire of the Holy Spirit, let the soul ties be broken in the name of Jesus. I disconnect my soul and my mind from them, Lord God. I reject and rebuke the spirit of lust that developed from fornicating with these men. Father, purify my mind, my body, and spirit in the mighty name of Jesus. Amen."

Meditate the same scripture above and while doing so, go to YouTube and in the search bar type "Withholding Nothing Medley by William McDowell lyrics."

CONFESSION TO CHRIST:

On the next blank page, in 5 sentences tell The Lord how grateful you are for giving you the grace to make it this far. Start with: *"Father, I come humbly before Your throne to say thank You…"*

This completes Day 5!

CONFESSIONS TO JESUS:

_____

_____

_____

_____

_____

_____

_____

_____

_____

_____

_____

_____

_____

_____

_____

_____

_____

_____

_____

_____

_____

_____

_____

_____

_____

_____

_____

_____

DAY 6: BE OBEDIENT

Good Morning, Overcomer! You are basically one day from completing week one! Today you will mostly meditate the word of God.

You can convince yourself that God doesn't care if you have premarital sex, but only if you ignore the Scripture. Don't be fooled and consumed by the sexual content that you see on social media, television and magazines today. All these things will surely pass away. If you were to die today, would you make it to heaven and would The Lord say to you "Well done"?

One of the things that I have come to realize in my 6 years of celibacy is that if I had waited until marriage, I would not have fought the spiritual battles that I did. I would have saved myself from being emotionally attached to my exes and being driven by negative forces that only came in existence when I welcomed it. NONE of this was healthy. NONE of it was honorable. I made the choice to sleep with them. I made the decision to allow my body and flesh to lead me astray even when I knew very well that it was no good to my soul. But we serve such an awesome and merciful God who saves us daily even when we don't want to save ourselves.

Can you image where I would be today if I was still a fornicator? Can you image how contaminated my soul would be? Can you image how broken my soul would still be? Can you also image how many souls would still be lost because I didn't write this book? How many women would still be bound in sexual sin?

It is indeed incredible what The Lord does for us when we are obedient to Him. I made a vow to surrender my body to Him as a living sacrifice and decided to become celibate. He then blessed me with a vision to first create an online course in June of 2016. A course with 21 modules that would help over 200 women become free and delivered from fornication and sexual bondage. Later, He then assigned me to turn the online course into a book. This very book that you are reading today. He truly rewards those that are faithful to Him.

"Whatever you do, work at it with all your heart, as working for the Lord, not for human masters, since you know that you will receive an inheritance from the Lord as a reward. It is the Lord Christ you are serving" **(Colossians 3:23-24)**.

MORNING:

Take your communion before you begin your day. You are going to meditate on these scriptures every 5 hours today. Set an alarm on your phone as a friendly reminder.

Corinthians 6:9 *"Don't you know that wicked people won't inherit the kingdom of God? Stop deceiving yourselves! People who continue to commit sexual sins, worship false gods, commit adultery, homosexuals, thieves, those who are greedy or drunk, abusive language, or who rob people, will not inherit the kingdom of God."*

1 Corinthians 6:18-19 *"Run from sexual sin! No other sin as clearly affects the body as this one does. For sexual immorality is a sin against your own body. Don't you realize that your body is the temple of the Holy Spirit, who lives in you and was given to you by God? You do not belong to yourself."*

1 Thessalonians 4:3-4 *"God's will be for you to be holy, so stay away from all sexual sin. Then each of you will control his own body and live in holiness and honor."*

1 Corinthians 5:9-11 *"Do not associate with people who indulge in sexual sin. But I'm not talking about unbelievers who indulge in sexual sin, or are greedy or cheat people, or worship idols. You would have to leave this world to avoid people like that. What I am voicing is that you are not to associate with anyone who claims to be a believer, yet indulges in sexual sin, greedy, worships false idols, abusive, a drunkard, or cheats people. Don't even eat with such people."*

EVENING ASSIGNMENT:

Take a shower or bath tonight when you are finished, go on YouTube and in the search for "Fill Me Up & Over Flow Tasha Cobbs Lyrics" and apply the anointing oil all over your body again. While you are doing this, say this prayer:

Lord Jesus, I thank You for renewing my body and establishing me in the Kingdom. The enemy of sexual perversion no longer has control over my life. He has no ground to operate sexually because I am no longer a fornicator. My mind has been renewed and my spirit is being transformed. I will never go back where I was. I am completely disconnected from my past and the damage it did to me. You are my repairer and restorer. Thank You, Jesus, for delivering me. I owe You my entire life. As I sleep tonight, release Your angels to preserve me and keep me. In the name of Jesus Christ, Amen!"

CONFESSION TO CHRIST:

On the next blank page, in 5 sentences or more, tell The Lord what you know about your worth in Him. Start it with: *"Father, I am honored to be a daughter of Your Kingdom. I know my worth because...."*

This completes Day 6.

CONFESSIONS TO JESUS:

_____
_____
_____
_____
_____
_____
_____
_____
_____
_____
_____
_____
_____
_____
_____
_____
_____
_____
_____
_____
_____
_____
_____
_____
_____
_____
_____
_____
_____

DAY 7: THE HOUSE OF THE LORD

MORNING:

Good morning, Overcomer! I love Sunday mornings! If you were not able to go to church Friday night, this is your opportunity to do so. But before you start, take your communion and go on YouTube. In the search bar type "Only You Are Holy by Donnie McClurkin." Let the song play as you say this powerful prayer:

"Father God, in the mighty name of Jesus, Lord I thank You for this day. Thank You for allowing me to live by Your grace. Thank You for this journey that is reshaping my spiritual life and getting me closer to You. Father, I don't want anything in my life that does not please You. Order my steps and continue to lead me as I am completely lost without You. As I embark on today's assignment regarding this journey, give me the strength and peace to complete everything today. Destroy and block every distraction from friends and people that will be sent to me by the enemy. I don't want to lose focus. I don't

want to go astray."

Before you leave the house to go to church, take that sheet of paper that has all the names you listed and write on top of it "The soul ties are broken in Jesus' name." Have a seed ready (regardless of the amount) and put both the seed and the sheet of paper in an envelope. Before you enter into the house of The Lord, expect that He will touch you and have faith that you will not return home the same. During service, if there is an altar call, answer the call and rededicate your life to God. If you feel like kneeling, down kneel down, if you want to cry, cry. This is between you and God. The people that are watching you don't matter. They did not create you nor do they have anything to do with your soul. This is a very spiritual exercise that you are doing and you will reap its fruit in due time. Make sure to leave the envelope at the altar.

If it's allowed, stay a little longer on the altar after service and spend time with The Lord in prayer. Declare this while you are at the altar:

"Father I come before you through Your glory and grace. I am here in Your House. Thank You for this amazing opportunity to honor You. Thank You for changing me during this journey. I repent for all the sin I have committed from the day I was born. Forgive me for being disobedient with Your Word. Thank you for a second chance. A chance to walk in purity and holiness. I love You and I will continue to honor You with my body as a living sacrifice. In Jesus' name. Amen."

When you get home you are going to do a spiritual house cleaning. I know that during the fast you got rid of all the sex toys and explicit sexual content from all your gadgets. This time you are going to get rid of all the gifts that you received from your exes. Yes, from the panties to the pricy jewelry! You are going to throw them away regardless of their value and how expensive they are. Attaching yourself to these things also gives room for the enemy to operate in the area of soul ties. Get rid of all the provocative clothes that are too revealing and scream out "SEX" and "LUST." These attires are inappropriate and as daughter of King Jesus, you should not wear them. Do the same with your car. Get rid of everything in there that your ex gave you. What's in the trunk, girl? One last thing that you should get rid of is the mattress that you used when you fornicated. Maybe not today, but definitely soon enough when you can.

SCRIPTURE:

Meditate this word every 5 hours all day today. Set up an alarm on your phone as a reminder. Don't forget to mediate at work as well.

Isaiah 43:29 *"See, I am doing a new thing! Now it springs up; do you not see it? I am making a way in the wilderness and streams in the wasteland."*

You will meditate on this scripture all day as much as possible. Set an alarm on your phone as a reminder, if you must!

EVENING ASSIGNMENTS:

Before you sleep tonight, take a nice warm shower or bath again. Go to YouTube and in the search bar type: "I won't go back lyrics William McDowell." Apply the anointed oil on your entire body and make this declaration:

"Thank You Lord for closing this chapter in my life! I am no longer attached to my ex-lovers, ex sexual partners. I renounce everything that worked against me sexually with my spirit through the gifts that they gave me. My home is cleansed by the blood of Jesus.

My car is cleansed by the blood of The Lamb. I am being made new. I was bought with the price. From this day forward, no devil in hell, no demon, will pull me back into my past. I will not go back to the way things used to be. In the name of Jesus, I command that the soul ties are broken. The soul ties that were formed through sexual intercourse, oral sex, pornography and masturbation, are destroyed in the name of Jesus. Amen."

CONFESSION TO CHRIST:

You have completed week 1. You should have so much to tell The Lord tonight. On the next blank page, in 5 to 8 sentences reflect on everything that happened on this journey this week. Talk to Jesus and start it with: *"Dear Lord. I am so grateful that I have completed week one. These last seven days were…"*

This completes Day 7.

CONFESSIONS TO JESUS:

DAY 8: A LIVING SACRIFICE

MORNING:

Good morning, Overcomer! Take your communion and say this prayer:

"Lord, I bless You for another week. I commit my thoughts, emotions, actions and intentions into Your graceful hands. Father, shower me with Your glory. Give me supernatural strength to overcome every sexual temptation and vulnerability. Let my mind be aligned with Your Word, Father. No sexual demon has the power to control my mind, in the name of Jesus. No ex of mine has the power to pull me back in the name of Jesus. I pray for the atmosphere to become conducive right now, so Holy Spirit come. Take over my entire day. Let Your Gracious Spirit, Lord, lead every step that I take today. I will not fail, in the name of Jesus Christ. Father, I thank You for answering this prayer, in the name of Jesus. Amen."

Fornication is a form of sexual sin or immorality that involves voluntary sexual relation between two people who are not married to each other—and the couple could be of opposite or same sex. God does not condone such an act regardless of our liberal views in the 21st century. Fornication is the outright breaking of God's Word and His judgment awaits the impenitent.

Clearly, God will judge all who live in sexual immorality; whether that is fornicating or committing adultery. Paul says that *"fornication and all uncleanness or covetousness, let it not even be named among you, as is fitting for saints"* **(Ephesians 5:3)**. God has the final word on this, I don't. **Revelation 21:8** reveals, *"But the cowardly, the unbelieving, the vile, the murderers, the sexually immoral, those who practice magic arts, the idolaters and all liars—they will be consigned to the fiery lake of burning sulfur. This is the second death."*

EVENING ASSIGNMENT:

Before you sleep tonight, apply the anointing oil in your inner thighs and begin to worship King Jesus. Worship is the gateway to releasing blessings and angelic activities. Whenever I go days without spending time in worship, my spirit becomes filled with unease and my soul begins to cry out, because it's thirsty for it. One of my goals regarding this book is for the readers, like you, to build their worship experience.

While Jesus was at Jacob's well, He had an encounter with a Samaritan woman to whom He said, *"True worshipers will worship the Father in spirit and in truth, for they are the kind of worshipers the Father seeks. God is spirit, and his worshipers must worship in spirit and in truth."* In other translation, the term worship, especially in the Old Testament, means *"to touch the ground with the forehead."* On that note, worship is an act of *"reverence, veneration, adoration, and paying homage."* The object of worship is usually greater than the worshiper, whether acknowledged or not.

Unfortunately, going by the above facts, we often worship earthly things like luxury cars, sports, fashion, entertainment, celebrities, and even spirit beings **(See Exodus 20:3-6; Revelation 19:10)**. True, biblical, and reasonable worship has been defined in the Apostle Paul's letter, that you should *"present your bodies as a living sacrifice, holy and acceptable to God, which is your spiritual worship to God"* **(Romans 12:1)**. Sure, to worship anything other than God is idolatry. Are there any examples of acceptable worship in the Bible for our emulation?

Our God is most worthy of honor and praise, as He deserves to see us in His temple blessing Him for who He is and what He has done. Worship God in the temple of your body, at home, at work, everywhere you go.

PRAYER:

"Father, I love You and I desire more of You in my life Lord. Take away every fleshly desire in me that does not please You. Teach me how to be more like You so that I may be a light for others in darkness. Let Your Spirit fill me up until it overflows. Let it run over and never run dry. Let the rivers of living waters begin to operate in my life. Lead me to walk in Your light, lead me to be an example for others Lord. Take away every selfish desire that resides on the inside of me. You are my Lion of the Tribe of Judah, The Rose of Sharron, The lover of my soul. Receive my worship Father. May the fruit of my lips continue to adore You. I love You and I thank You for loving me unconditionally. You are the sweetest lover I have ever known. Amen."

CONFESSION TO CHRIST:

What was your experience like going to church yesterday? Overall, what has changed so far in your life because of it? On the next blank page, write to Jesus in 8 sentences telling him your experience. Starting with: *"Dear Father, I want to thank You for the opportunity to come into Your House and meet You there. The experience was…"*

This completes Day 8.

CONFESSIONS TO JESUS:

DAY 9: THE JOURNEY CONTINUES

MORNING:

Good morning, Overcomer! Welcome to another glorious day, triumphant people of God. You have attained a remarkable feat as you celebrate two weeks into the program, which is more reason why you must continue to persist. You must realize that you have accomplished so much over the past two weeks as you are gradually being transformed. I must encourage you to be steadfast and to continue doing good deeds.

Observe the communion and then search "Hezekiah Walker - Moving Forward Lyrics" in the search bar. Make this affirmation in faith:

"Lord, I thank You that I have made it this far. Thank you Father for not giving up on me. Thank You for the fire that is burning inside of me for You. Thank you for reminding me that I am precious and so important to you. In the name of The Lord Jesus

Christ, I will never go back. My past will never define me. My past will never block my future. I am where I am today because of Your love and grace Lord. The best days are ahead of me. My testimony will be greater than my setbacks, failures and fears. Jesus, you are the best thing that has ever happened to me. Thank You for removing every desire to fornicate. Thank You for consuming my sexual appetite! I (say you name) am moving forward. (Begin to walk as you make the rest of the declarations). I am moving forward. Holy Spirit, you are ushering me into a realm of glory; A realm of honor, a realm of peace, joy and abundance. I will never be the same, in the name of Jesus."

BIBLE PASSAGE:

You will study and reflect on the Bible passage provided at every 5-hour interval. This should last the entire day. You must endeavor to reflect on the Bible passage even when at work.

Ecclesiastes 5:4 *"When you make a vow to God, don't delay in following through, for God takes no pleasure in fools. Keep all the promises you make to him."*

EVENING ASSIGNMENT:

Romans 12:1-2 *"I appeal to you therefore, brothers, by the mercies of God, to present your bodies as a living sacrifice, holy and acceptable to God, which is your spiritual worship. Do not be conformed to this world, but be transformed by the renewal of your mind, that by testing you may discern what is the will of God, what is good and acceptable and perfect."*

For an accurate knowledge of the word of God contained in the **Book of Romans 12:1-2**, I have prepared a detailed and orderly account that captures every aspect of this scripture in a way that bestows a perfect understanding which becomes light unto your feet. We will start by examining the concept of sacrificing to God which was described by

Apostle Paul in the book of Romans as "reasonable worship." For a proper understanding of the sacrificing to God, we would take a quick tour of the Old Testament where the parlance of "sacrifice" was first used. In the Old Testament you would find that sacrifice is a prerequisite for the true worship of God. Sacrificing to God was a sacred spiritual practice and a fundamental requirement that pleases the Lord. There are various spiritual importances of sacrificing to the Lord, as people scarified sheep, bulls, pigeons and other animals as a form of thanksgiving to the Lord. Sacrifices were made as offerings, repentance, and restoration, which is the focus of Paul's teaching in Romans chapter 12. The purpose of the sin offering or guilt offering (as it is referred to in some chapters) is to remove the sins from the people which would have been a hindrance to God's favor and would have provoked the fury of God.

In fact, guilt offering or sacrifice is meant to cleanse worshipers as the sacrificed animal would placate the anger of God while extricating worshipers from their misconducts and offenses.

While this was used to manage the guilt and sins of sinners and alleviating the consequences, it was clear that the blood of animals could not remove sins. As this was expressly stated in the book of Hebrew 10:14. It is clear, however, that the sacrifice of animals for the atonement of sins was a way to reduce the repercussions and ramifications of sins. It is also clear that the sacrifice of animals in the Old Testament was used as a representation of the ultimate futuristic occurrence which has changed the fate of humanity forever. It is and was the greatest of all sacrifices; the sacrifice of Jesus Christ which is the price for redemption. The sacrifice of Jesus Christ the Son of God, which takes away the sin of the world.

When Apostle Paul talks about presenting our body as a living sacrifice, holy and acceptable to God, some of us get terrified at the meaning. While others are simply uncertain of what this statement implies. However, for a proper understanding we must carefully examine the book of **Romans 12:1-2** for a clear understanding.

Presenting our bodies to God means that we offer our body to Him. You must offer your body to the Lord because He is the owner of your body. The scripture makes us to understand that our body is the temple of the Lord. Also, the Bible tells us in the book of Corinthian 6:20 that you were bought with a price therefore honor God with your bodies. From the aforesaid, it is evident we are not expected to sacrifice our body for sin, as Jesus Christ has paid the ultimate sacrifice for all of our sins. However, we are expected to walk in the light of this knowledge by being holy in our ways. It becomes clear that we are now expected to live in righteousness and in the knowledge that our body has been bought with a price and must be kept holy. The sacrifice talked about is the sacrifice of holiness and righteousness which is corroborated by Apostle Peter in **1 Peter 2-5**.

You must understand therefore that your holiness is a filthy rag before God; however, through Jesus Christ your holiness would be completed and therefore acceptable to the Lord.

- **Lifestyle:** It is quite easy to make the erroneous impression that the statement that presents your bodies as a "living sacrifice." Requires that you should become a martyr like Stephen or give up yourself as a sacrifice like Jesus Christ. This is further from what the scripture says. When Apostle Paul said *"present your* *bodies as a living sacrifice,"* he simply meant that our way of life and character must mirror the life of Jesus Christ.

Your life should please God and be in accordance to his commandments. When you put God first in all of your ways, when you consider God in all of your undertakings, when you remember God in all of your intentions and thoughts, you have indeed accomplished what Apostle Paul said.

- **Righteousness:** When the scripture talks about *"present your bodies as a living sacrifice, holy and acceptable to God,"* it puts emphasis on the need to live in holiness and righteousness. We are expected to walk in the light of God and in the light of the knowledge that we have been purchased with the blood of Jesus Christ. Therefore, we must not defile our bodies with sin, but be transformed by the righteousness of Jesus Christ as is contained in the scripture which says *"Do not present your members to sin as instruments for unrighteousness, but present yourselves to God as those who have been brought from death to life, and your members to God as instruments for righteousness."* From the aforesaid, it is clear that reasonable worship is when our body is kept holy before God.

The righteousness that comes with *"present your bodies as a living sacrifice, holy and acceptable to God"* is not meant to halfhearted. The Lord requires total submission to him and his word. Also it should not be per-time surrender or a conditional surrender. You must surrender totally to God in the Knowledge that you brought from death to life.

This is "reasonable worship."

With all of this in mind, we would now examine biblical ways on how to make our bodies perfect for reasonable worship:

- **Cleansing the earthly body:** The foremost step to preparing for "reasonable worship" is to cleanse our bodies. Cleansing our body does not mean having our bath or personal hygiene. Cleansing our earthly body means that we must keep our body holy by avoiding evil sights and listening to things that can corrupt us. What you see and what you hear can defile the body as such. This must be guarded. Remember the scripture says that we should guide our minds with all diligence for out of it are the issues of life.

- **Maintaining fitness and health:** Keeping your body healthy is an important requirement for "reasonable worship." Therefore, we are required to make sure that we are healthy and fit as this is the wish of God for us. He said in his word, *"beloved I wish above all things that thou mayest prosper and be in health even as thy soul prospereth."* Again, it is made apparent smoking, excessive drinking, bad eating habits and so on are not the will of God for our lives **(Ephesians 5:29)**. When we protect our body from harmful substances and practices we are in conformity with the requirements for "reasonable worship."

- **Take charge of your body:** Always take charge of your body as this is a fundamental requirement for "reasonable worship." While the body has a propensity towards sin, it is important that you exercise the authority giving to you, in the name of Jesus, and take charge of your body by aligning it with the will of God. This is contained in the book of **(1 Thessalonians 4:4)**.

Repentance from Sin

The first step to repentance is a proper understanding of yourself and this understanding would come when you provide sincere response these questions:

• How can you show respect God with your Body?

• What are the various approaches you can adopt in order to take charge of your body?

Now that you have an in-depth understanding of the word, *it is important that you put down the various benefits you have learned from the scripture.*

CONFESSIONS TO JESUS:

_____

_____

_____

_____

_____

_____

_____

_____

_____

_____

_____

_____

_____

_____

_____

_____

_____

_____

_____

_____

_____

_____

_____

_____

_____

_____

_____

_____

DAY 10: YOUR BODY IS A SACRED TEMPLE

MORNING:

Good morning, Overcomer. Take your communion and say this prayer: *"Father, have Your way in my life again. Thank You for the chance to live again. Thank You for Your mercy that is renewed this very morning. Have total control of my body, mind, spirit and soul. In Jesus' name, Amen."*

SCRIPTURE:

Meditate this word all day every 5 hours. Set an alarm on your phone as a reminder.

Matthew 15:19 *"For out of the heart come evil thoughts, murders, adulteries, fornications, thefts, false witness, slanders."*

1 Corinthians 5:9-11 *"I wrote before for you to not associate with immoral people;*

I did not at all mean with the immoral people of this world. Or with the covetous and swindlers, idolaters, fornicators; for then you would have to go out of the world. But actually, I told you not to associate with any so-called brother if he is an immoral person, covetous, an idolater, reviler, a drunkard, or a swindler—not even to eat with such a one."

HOW SOUL TIES ARE FORMED

I believe there are other ways by which soul ties are formed, but here are some that I am aware of.

Sexual relations: Godly soul ties are formed when a couple is married. **Ephesians 5:31**, *"For this cause shall a man leave his father and mother, and shall be joined unto his wife, and they two shall be one flesh,"* and the Godly soul tie between a husband and the wife that God intends for the couple is unbreakable by man **(Mark 10:7-9)**. However, when a person has ungodly sexual relations with another person, an ungodly soul tie is then formed. **1 Corinthians 6:16**, *"What? Know ye not that he which is joined to a harlot is one body? For two, saith he, shall be one flesh."* This soul tie fragments the soul, and is destructive. People who have many past relationships find it very difficult to 'bond' or be joined with another, because their soul is fragmented.

Steps to Breaking Soul Ties

1. **Repent of the sin of fornication if it is the cause in your case.** Don't excuse it. Sin is sin, and forgiveness only comes when you acknowledge it. Ask God to cleanse and justify you by the blood of the Lamb.

2. **Get rid of all items you received from your sex partner, no matter how precious the gifts might be.** Don't tell yourself, "Oh, what a precious diamond ring!" Exchange of gifts serves as a seal to

the bond, the soul tie. Those greeting cards, flowers, fashion products, love letters, photos, and others, throw them away in the bin.

3. **Cut your ties with the sex partner.** In other words, don't be close friends again. Stop visiting and calls. But if the person is a member of your church, limit your contact to church; don't go to their home. As for co- workers in your workplace, let them know their limits. All these will keep you from falling into temptation.

4. **Renounce every word of promise, oath, agreement, and vow that you have made to the person.** Verbally renounce those so-called statements of love you have spoken under the pressure of your crush or lust for someone's body. Break the oath with another Bible- based statement in the name of Jesus. "In the name of Jesus, I renounce the word of oath, agreement, commitment and promise that I made to (name the person) when I told him/her that 'I'll never love anyone besides him/her…'"

5. **Forgive the person and forgive yourself.** Maybe you have developed a bitter, resentful spirit toward the other person. You must leave it to let God. Complete healing starts with receiving forgiveness from God when you let go of those hurtful feelings you have for the other. Forgive! Again, forgive yourself for walking into the arms of a strange person God didn't intend for you as a partner. "For Christ's sake, I forgive so-and-so for…"

6. **Renounce all soul ties.** *"In the name of Jesus, I renounce all ungodly soul ties formed between (name the person) and myself when we had (name the sin)."*

7. **Finally, break the soul ties.** Using the power of the name and the blood of Jesus, command the bond to break and release your soul. *"In Jesus' name, I break the ungodly soul ties formed between (name the person) and myself because of our (name the sins)."*

Demons of Fornication

In the previous section, we didn't talk about getting ourselves freed from evil spirits. In **Hosea 5:3-4**, we read about the spirit (demon) of fornication. So it's not enough to break the soul ties, it's essential you receive deliverance from those demons too. Before going into that, let's look at some other manifestations of this spirit.

1. Incubus: it's an evil spirit that sleeps with women while they are asleep. It's a sexual demon in the masculine form.
2. Succubus: this is a sexual demon in the feminine form that comes to have sexual intercourse with men when asleep.

EVENING ASSIGNMENT:

Just spend 15 minutes in worship tonight! You read so much today already.

CONFESSION TO CHRIST:

On the next blank page, *what advice would you give your 15-year-old son about premarital sex?*

This completes DAY 10!

CONFESSIONS TO JESUS:

_____

_____

_____

_____

_____

_____

_____

_____

_____

_____

_____

_____

_____

_____

_____

_____

_____

_____

_____

_____

_____

_____

_____

_____

_____

_____

DAY 11: BEING SINGLE IS HARD

MORNING:

Good morning, Overcomer! Take your communion and before you begin to pray this morning, I want to share something with you. There are going to be times where the enemy will use someone to cause you to lose focus and get out of line in this spiritual journey. Your co-worker might do something that will drive you up the wall and make you say something ungodly to them. A customer will say something that makes you want to pull you hair out and respond with an attitude. I say this this to say that you should be very alert when the enemy is at work. His main goal is to distract you, frustrate you and shift your focus so you can lose sight of this spiritual journey and literally fail. This is why it's important that prayer should be part of your lifestyle automatically. It should be an everyday thing. It should be done like how you take a shower every day. He is the word; the word is Him.

Now that I have shared that with you, dive in His presence and say this prayer:

"Father, I thank You again for this new day. I am blessed to be called Your daughter. Thank You for giving me another chance to be in Your presence. In the name of The Lord Jesus, I destroy the assignment that the enemy has calculated to use people to distract me and cause me to go astray. This assignment will not stand. This assignment is canceled by the blood of Jesus. I commend my flesh to also subdue and for my spirit to be empowered. May the blood of Jesus Christ cover me against all demonic weapons and satanic arrows of distraction, in Jesus' name. Amen!"

SCRIPTURE:

Revelation 21:8 *"But the fearful, and unbelieving, and the abominable, and murderers, and whoremongers, and sorcerers, and idolaters, and all liars, shall have their part in the lake which burned with fire and brimstone: which is the second death."*

You will meditate on this scripture all day as much as possible. Set an alarm on your phone as a reminder, if you must!

EVENING ASSIGNMENTS:

Go on YouTube and in the search bar, type "To Worship You I Live-Israel and New Breed."

Being single is hard.

Having observed the loneliness of Adam in the Garden of Eden, God said to Himself, *"It is not good for the man to be alone. I will make a helper suitable for him."* **(Genesis 2:18)** A woman was then made for him to address the man's need for companionship. The two then came into lifelong marital union. Without doubts, marriage is an established institution in the Bible, though the New Testament is positive about being single. In marriage, our desire for intimacy is fulfilled and therefore, singles are more prone to loneliness and sexual temptations. Some get married to avoid such tendencies, while some choose to be celibate, maybe because of their personality, physical conditions, or sexual orientation. For people who decide to remain single, they will likely have intense struggle with loneliness and temptations.

Now, loneliness and sexual temptation go hand in hand. Lonely people are more susceptible to sexual fantasy because their drive for intimacy may cause them to resort to sexual acts that contradict God's will. If you're in this situation, pray lest you fall into sin. Here is a word of wisdom: if you choose to be single, be it in short or long term, try to fill your need for companionship through other relationships—with friends, relatives, coworkers, etc., though with caution when you are dealing with non-relatives. Avoid being alone; be accountable to someone.

Being single is temporal.

Singles of today will get married someday, though others will remain single for life. But, I will say, no Christian is single forever. Acts of marriage is a picture of the union between Christ and His Church...forever. He is the Bridegroom coming for His Bride, the Church. *"Let us rejoice and be glad and give him glory! For the wedding of the Lamb has come, and his bride has made herself ready"* **(Revelation 7:17; 19:7)**. On the day of His arrival, all pain and sorrow we have ever had in life will be history—gone with the past, and forgotten. Shouts of joy will fill your mouth!

A lady once exclaimed after we had a conversation about heaven, saying,

"I can't wait for my wedding!" Let's all share the same hope no matter how difficult our lives may be now. Having relationships with fellow humans is good, but not as great as having an intimate union with Christ here on earth though the indwelling of the Holy Spirit in our lives. And nothing surpasses our eternal relationship with Him. We thank God for the gift of celibacy. Are you single now? Accept it as a gift from the Lord and maximize it to His glory in all things.

Strive to be godly. Being single makes you susceptible to living the self-centered life of a recluse— in thought or deed. This can engender sexual fantasy, which may even lead you into the actual act as you seek to satisfy your urge for intimacy. Be accountable to reliable people around you.

Don't lose your focus on heaven—keep your eyes on the goal. Your eternal union with Christ matters a lot.

CONFESSION TO JESUS:

On the next blank page write a letter to Jesus about how you feel about being single and if you are struggling, tell Him what you want Him to do for you. Start the letter with *"Dear Lord, being single is/has been..."*

This completes day 11.

CONFESSIONS TO JESUS:

DAY 12: LEAVING UNGODLY FRIENDS BEHIND

MORNING:

Happy Friday, Overcomer! Take your communion before you begin your day. I will get straight to the point. The weekend is approaching again. Don't give into temptation. Don't find yourself at places the Lord would not be pleased with. Don't hang out with people that will contaminate your soul. You are on a spiritual journey and you cannot behave as those in the world! You are set apart! At this point, you really should no longer have contact with those individuals anyway! This was part of your assignment in week 1. What you are doing is going to birth fruit and you will look back and thank The Lord when it is all done.

Say this prayer:

"Lord Jesus, I thank You for the strength that you are giving me each day! I thank You for the grace that You have made available to me so freely. I thank You for changing me and shaping me into the woman You created me to be. I thank You for breaking down the walls of bitterness and resentment. Thank You for delivering my mind from demonic bombardment and lies of the enemy. You are my deliverer and I am grateful. I give you my entire life. Have Your way today. In Jesus' name. Amen."

SCRIPTURE:

1 John 2:15-17 *"Do not love this world nor the things it offers you, for when you love the world, you do not have the love of the Father in you. For the world offers only a craving for physical pleasure, a craving for everything we see, and pride in our achievements and possessions. These are not from the Father, but are from this world. And this world is fading away, along with everything that people crave. But anyone who does what pleases God will live forever."*

EVENING:

So it is Friday night and the temptation is real. You want to go out, but you know your friends are of bad influence! Or you want to "chill" with that man, but you know it will lead to fornication. I want to challenge you to do something that sounds insane. Go to your favorite restaurant by yourself and go on a date with The King, Jesus Himself. Yes, you may look crazy sitting all by yourself at that table, but so what? You aren't there to please anybody. Sit like a princess before your Father and enjoy a nice light meal (remember we are still fasting on fruits and veggies, so try to eat light). The purpose of this is to remind you that you don't need a man to take you out to eat in order to be content. You don't need a man that will smoothly lavish you with expensive meals and gifts just to make his way into his bed or your bed with him. If you can't afford to go out tonight or just don't have time, go to YouTube and in the search bar type in "NO MORE SHEETS - Juanita Bynum" and I encourage you to fast forward the video to "20:00."

CONFESSIONS TO CHRIST:

Pretend you are a mother of a 14-year-old daughter. What would you tell her about sex? On the following blank page, *write her a 5 sentence letter (including scripture)*. The scripture is not part of the 5 sentences.

This concludes DAY 12!

CONFESSIONS TO JESUS:

DAY 13: YOUR WORTH AND SELF-ESTEEM

MORNING:

Good morning, Overcomer! Remaining celibate until you get married has many benefits that the devil doesn't want people to know today. Don't be deceived. The best thing, the right thing, the biblical thing to do is to wait until you're married—your body is too precious to be sexually used and dumped by those guys out there. Stay clear of STDs, shame, guilt, and unwanted pregnancy. You can't afford to have an abortion and it's against God's word. God blessings are reserved for marriage. To access them, keep yourself for your God-given spouse. Never follow the ideals of the world about love & relationships.

Say this prayer:

"In the mighty name of The Lord Jesus, I commend the flesh of mine to be subdued. I

commend you to be overruled by The Holy Spirit today. I refuse to talk about sex, think about sex or engage in any sexual activity. I train my mind to only think Godly thoughts, in the name of Jesus. I rebuke every temptation and lustful offer. I bind and reject it all in the name of The Lord Jesus. FIRE OF THE HOLY SPIRIT ENTER MY BODY RIGHT NOW! Paralyze very sexual demon and desire. Overturn evil errors released to distract me from my journey, in The name of Jesus. I will not give up. I will not go back. Father, I thank you for preserving me with Your precious blood. In Jesus' name, Amen!"

SCRIPTURE

Meditate on this scripture all day.

1 Thessalonians 4:3-4 *"God's will is for you to be holy, so stay away from all sexual sin. Then each of you will control his own body and live in holiness and honor."*

EVENING ASSIGNMENT:

Relax; go on YouTube and in the search bar type: "Fill Me Up & Over Flow by Tasha Cobbs with Lyrics." This might sound ridiculous but it's necessary that you do this! Stand in front of your mirror completely naked. Look in the mirror and bless your body with positive words. You have probably been used and abused to the point where you have lost your self-esteem and confidence. You have lost your self-worth due to what the men in your life said to you in the past. They mistreated you. They verbally abused you and you have never healed from it. Tonight, you are going to destroy low self-esteem by this powerful prayer! Speak these holy words to your body out loud:

"In the name of Jesus, BODY OF MINE, you are the temple of the Holy Spirit. Body of mine, you were perfectly made in the image of GOD! Body of mine, you will not allow any men to again abuse you, hurt you, use you and mistreat you. On this day, I

promise you, for the rest of my life that I will guard you from hurt, pain abuse and harm. I rebuke every spirit of low-self-esteem, lack of confidence that was developed due to harsh words that were spoken to you. From today, I promise to love you deeper, take care of you each day and appreciate you every second. I REJECT EVERY ABUSIVE WORD THAT WAS SPOKEN OVER YOU. I REBUKE EVERY INSULT AND EVERY CURSE THAT WAS SPOKEN OVER YOU. Now, in the name of Jesus, body of mine, I command you to align with the word of God. You will not fall into temptation and allow any man to have sex with you without first marrying you. You, body of mine, you are beautiful, you are precious, and you carry the crown of glory. You will not attract ungodly men that will take advantage of you. You, body of mine, I love you and I will take care of you because you belong to my Savior Jesus and whatever belongs to Him must be well taken care of! Body of mine, I bless you; I break every ungodly soul tie that has attached itself to you. I disconnect you from sexual desires and lustful acts. Body of mine, you belong to Christ. Body of mine, you are blessed and not cursed in Jesus' name Amen!"

CONFESSIONS TO CHRIST:

We all have body features that we certainly love. Mine are my nose, toes, smile and hair. On the following blank page, write a 5 to 8 sentence letter to Jesus telling him what part of you that you appreciate and love most. Of course we are grateful for every part of our body, each part serves its purpose but there are just a few that we appreciate a little more. Start the letter with *"Dear Jesus, thank you for creating me perfectly in Your image…"*

This concludes Day 13.

CONFESSIONS TO JESUS:

DAY 14: BE BOLD FOR CHRIST

MORNING:

Good morning, Overcomer! Take your communion as you begin your day. Say this prayer:

"Lord Jesus, I am grateful that You have been with me in this life transforming journey. I am excited to have made it to the end of the second week. I pray for those that are lost Father, I pray that You are going to use me to deliver them from fornication because You are setting me free. I am no longer ignorant of the devices of the enemy; such as masturbation, sex toys or pornography. All those things are filthy and the tools of the enemy to keep me in bondage. NOTHING in this world will (again) separate me from You. Nothing in this world is worth me spending eternity in hell with sexual demons. NOTHING in this world today will ever come between us. Jesus, Father, continue to give me grace to walk in purity and righteousness, in Jesus' name. Amen!"

Today, I want you to go to church   and spend time in His House. Spend time in the presence of our Father. If you cannot go this morning, attend an evening service. Share your testimony about how the Lord is changing your life from a being fornicator to a woman of holiness and purity. I know this will take a lot of courage and tenacity. Encourage others to stop fornicating and refer to **Thessalonians 4:3-4**, *"God's will is for you to be holy, so stay away from all sexual sin. Then each of you will control his own body and live in holiness and honor."*

I know it will take boldness for you to stand in front of the congregation and share your journey. Have no fear in sharing the marvelous thing that The Lord is doing in your life. By doing this, you will save someone's soul today. **Revelation 12:11** says, *"We shall overcome by the blood of the lamb and by the word of our testimonies."*

EVENING ASSIGNMENT:

The second assignment for today is for you to call or text someone that you know needs to stop fornicating. Find someone that you know is on the road to hell because of her sexual lifestyle, someone that you deeply care about that you know needs to be delivered from this sexual addiction. Be bold and if this friendship or relationship ends because you spoke God's word over their lives, then let it be! It is better to save a soul than let it go straight to hell especially if the Lord is setting you free from that SAME sin! Talk to them about soul- ties and the consequences of fornication and sex before marriage.

What do you think would happen if you had a cure for cancerous growth and you kept it to yourself, from the sick ones? If a truck was about to crush a toddler in a pram by the roadside where you were, would you just

126

look on? If you wouldn't keep quiet in either case, then those of us that have escaped eternal damnation through salvation in Jesus Christ can't afford to keep the message from others. Some people even claim that our primary duty is not to win souls for the Lord but to glorify Him. I wouldn't argue on theological propositions, but then they need to realize that God is glorified when we bring forth *"much fruit"* **(John 15:8)**. The truth is, when you win people to the Lord, or bring them to church, or when you share testimonies of conversion with others, believers would be inspired and glorified God. Then they would be encouraged to do the same.

SCRIPTURE:

1 Corinthians 6:18-19 *"Run from sexual sin! No other sin as clearly affects the body as this one does. For sexual immorality is a sin against your own body. Don't you realize that your body is the temple of the Holy Spirit, who lives in you and was given to you by God? You do not belong to yourself."*

CONFESSION TO JESUS:

On the following blank page write a letter to Jesus. Tell Him whatever comes to mind this very moment. *How are you feeling? How has this experience been so far?* You have come to the conclusion of week 2, I am sure you have a handful to say to Him, so write your heart out! Start with *"Dear Jesus, Wow…"*

This concludes Day 14.

CONFESSIONS TO JESUS:

DAY 15: THE LORD RESTORES

MORNING:

Good morning, Overcomer! Take your communion and say this prayer:

"Father, I am just grateful to be alive. Thank You for providing me with a roof over my head and for just loving me unconditionally. This has been such an amazing and life changing experience. I no longer have the desire to fornicate, masturbate, or even watch pornography. Lord, you have delivered me from that stubborn stronghold. Please increase my strength this week, continue to help me as I desire more of You. I don't ever want to live my life without You. You are forever the love of my soul. Let you blood cover me today and protect me from every attack of the enemy. In Jesus' name, Amen."

1 Corinthians 6:18-19 *"Run from sexual sin! No other sin so clearly affects the body as this one does. For sexual immorality is a sin against your own body. Don't you realize that your body is the temple of the Holy Spirit, who lives in you and was given to* *you by God? You do not belong to yourself."*

Take 10 minutes to worship our Lord with this song. Go to YouTube, in the search bar type "What Can I Do by Tye Tribbett Lyrics."

You cannot live without Him. There is no peace or life of abundance without Him. Worship our Father and give it all to Him. You cannot make it on your own. Begin to pour out your heart to him. Adore Him with the fruit of your lips.

You are maybe still holding on to your past! You're still holding on to the text messages, pictures, and phone numbers of your exes. You're still holding on to the contact of that man that always calls you or text you only for sex. Delete all of this today. You cannot move forward with the same baggage. The Lord wants you to experience a new chapter where true love will actually find you! Maybe you are still "hoping" that after the journey, things can still "work out" with that man. NO, LET HIM GO! The Lord has a good man for you, but only if you are obedient and consider His divine instructions! How can you have something that you have never had before if you keep the same old things?

EVENING ASSIGNMENT & SCRIPTURE:

Isaiah 43:19 *"See, I am doing a new thing! Now it springs up; do you not perceive it? I am making a way in the wilderness and streams in the wasteland."*

When you hear the word new, it sounds great and exciting. It could suggest access to a potential opportunity, or an adventure into the unknown. It sometimes sounds like a terrain, a place, a situation you've never known before; and it connotes "change" as well. At the extreme, it might tend to instill fear in your mind.

As you step into a new season today, reassure yourself that you won't fear the unknown, but hope in the known—God and His Word. That's the anchor for your soul. God brings forth a new beginning to each of His children for a good purpose. Rest assured that since He is the author of new things, the new season comes with abundance of goodness for you **(James 1:17)**.

New is God's promise to you; He says to forget the former things because He will do a new thing and now it shall spring forth. God never fails; all His promises are yea and amen in Christ Jesus **(1 Corinthians 1:20)**. The greatest promise is in our hope that Christ's coming for us one day, and He will make all things new—new heaven and new earth **(Revelation 21:5)**. However, while we're still on earth waiting for Him, He is still in the business of doing new things for the good of His children, for His glory. Now, let's consider some instances of His work in this respect.

God Restores

God's supernatural ability to restore is most fascinating to me. Through the finished redemptive work of Christ, He restores the relationship Adam lost in the Garden to humankind by way of forgiveness and justification. This act is proof of His abundant mercy toward humanity. If He could do that, then He is able to restore broken hearts—or homes. He can restore our lost virtues and the years that have been lost to the impact of our sinful nature **(Joel 2:25)**. God can redeem the past, the present, and the future for you because He is not limited by time and space—He fills all eternity, from the beginning to the end.

On several occasions, we see God's power bring restoration to people. For Jacob, after he reunited with Joseph in Egypt, he considered his past "few and evil" days. But at his old age, he looked back and saw that God had always been his shepherd all along and that he had been delivered from the evil he once had in his life. **(Genesis 47:9; 48:15-16)** For Ruth, God took a family name on the verge of extinction and restored hope and a glorious future to them—the family eventually got into the lineage of the Messiah, Jesus.

In His days, Jesus Christ had a ministry of restoration. He restored the walking ability of the crippled, the sight of the blind, hearing to the deaf, speech to the dumb and new health to the diseased. **(Mark 8:22-26; Matthew 9:2-8; Mark 7: 31-37; Luke 5:12-25)** He didn't just heal their condition but restored life, hope, comfort, health, and security to broken people.

Has God restored anything to you? What are your expectations from God in the new season?

CONFESSION TO JESUS:

On the following blank page, write a 5 to 8 sentence letter to Jesus. Begin the letter with *"Father, I thank for making things new in my life! Thank you because I am not who I used to be...."*

This concludes Day 15.

CONFESSIONS TO JESUS:

_____

_____

_____

_____

_____

_____

_____

_____

_____

_____

_____

_____

_____

_____

_____

_____

_____

_____

_____

_____

_____

_____

_____

_____

_____

_____

DAY 16: YOUR NEW IDENTITY IN CHRIST

MORNING:

Good morning, Queen! Take your communion and begin your day with this prayer:

"In the name of The Lord Jesus, I will never go back to where I was and to who I was. Father I thank You for this new day. Bless me as I continue to embark on this journey. Fill my mind with Your thoughts. I cast down all my worries before You. I begin this day with acknowledging that you are indeed in total control I am no longer consumed by sexual desires and temptations in the name of Jesus. Father, take the wheel today. Invade my territory. Amen."

You need Him right now. You need Him today. Cry out to Him this morning and get His attention. I remember in 2010 how this song ministered to me so powerfully during my divorce. It became my worship melody for months and months. Connect with Him this morning. Go to YouTube. In the search bar type "Smokie Norful- I Need You Now Lyrics."

SCRIPTURE:

1 Thessalonians 4: 3-4 *"God's will is for you to be holy, so stay away from all sexual sin. Then each of you will control his own body and live in holiness and honor."*

EVENING ASSIGNMENT:

The Lord Renames

Names usually come with great significance in the Bible. The name of a person is oftentimes tied to their destiny. Eve means *"the mother of all the living"* Samuel means *"asked of God"* **(Genesis 3:20; 1 Samuel 1:20)**.

Another significant practice or event in the Bible accounts has to do with God giving people a new name. Receiving a new name from the Lord was a token of renewed covenant, renewed purpose, and a redeemed life. For instance, Abram became Abraham, Sarai became Sarah, Simon became Peter, and Saul became Paul **(Genesis 17:5; Matthew 4:18; Acts 13:9)**. When God redeemed and restored Israel to right standing with Himself, God gave the people a new name to demonstrate His love for them **(Hosea 1-2)**. In all this, all of these individuals and God's people— Israelites— received new identities when they forsook their old path of life to accept God as their LORD.

Although you may not receive a new name—in the natural—when you become a Christian, you do receive a new name in the spirit; you've accepted a new nature and a new identity. You are cleansed and made pure— white as snow—through the blood of Jesus. Now you put on

Christ's righteousness; you have to walk in it.

With a new chapter opened for you, you can now rest in the new identity you have in Christ. Regardless of your past failures, you are covered by God's mercies every day **(Lamentations 3:22-23)**.

Being in Christ gives you a new name, a new identity—a child of God, a Christian. Can you prove—by word and deed—that you're living out your new identity with purpose of mind? Where are your fruits?

CONFESSIONS TO CHRIST:

On the following blank page, write a letter to your "past," NOT to your ex, but to your past. Start the letter with: *"Dear Past, you no longer have power over me..."*

Before you sleep tonight, anoint your entire body with the anointing oil and declare the following prayer:

"Father God. I thank You for making me a new creation in You. Father, I thank You for this opportunity to rededicate my life back to You, God. You are so faithful for picking me up from where I fell so short of Your glory. Father, again, I present my body to You, Lord. Father, it is Yours. Let no temptation pull me back into sin. Give me the strength to not allow any man to lay me down for sex unless he is my husband. Lord Jesus, place the fear of the Lord in me. I want to be afraid to sin. I want to be so in love with You that NO other man could win my heart unless he is first in love with You! Lord, give me the spirit of discernment to quicken my spirit as soon as counterfeit is presented before me. Let my spirit be alert and turn away. Right away! Keep strange men away from me each day of my life. Wherever I go, let them NOT locate me. Let all the wrong men be far from me in Jesus' name. Father, present to me only the one You have

destined for me! Amen!"

This concludes Day 16.

CONFESSIONS TO JESUS:

_____
_____
_____
_____
_____
_____
_____
_____
_____
_____
_____
_____
_____
_____
_____
_____
_____
_____
_____
_____
_____
_____
_____
_____
_____
_____
_____
_____

DAY 17: THE CHAINS ARE BROKEN

MORNING:

Good morning, Overcomer! Take your communion before you start your day. Look how far you have made it in the journey. There are only 4 more days left! The purpose of the 21-day journey was designed to help you become celibate; help you understand the consequences of fornication; get you through deliverance so that you can continue on this journey until marriage. It is the Lord's desire for you to continue to walk in holiness and purity as you honor Him with your body! This journey will continue on and until your wedding night.

Say this prayer:

"There is power in the name of Jesus. Lord Your name is delivering me. Your name has set me free. Jesus Your name is the ONLY name that the enemy fears. By calling

Your name chains fall, demons tremble and evil spirits are destroyed! Father, in the name of Jesus, destroy every wicked scheme of the devil today. Destroy witchcraft and demonic conspiracy released to set me up in sexual sin. Let Your fire travel and consume every spirit of depression, low self-esteem, bitterness and unforgiveness. I AM FREE in Jesus' name! AMEN!"

Go to YouTube, in the search bar type: "Tasha Cobbs - Break Every Chain." The Lord has instructed that you anoint your feet with the communion and anointing oil. Then make this declaration as you apply the holy elements to your beautiful feet:

"In the name of the Lord Jesus! Father, by this oil, I command every chain that has held my feet in sexual sin including masturbation and pornography, to break in the name of Jesus. I declare that my feet will walk in holiness, honor, and in the fear of the Lord. In the name of Jesus, my feet will not lead me in temptation. My feet shall be led by God. My feet shall be ordered by the Lord. From today, I shall walk in favor, peace, glory, joy, and honor. Because my feet are standing in the Word of God, I will not stumble nor fall into any sexual trap. Because my feet are anointed, I will never find myself sleeping with a man that is not my husband. In Jesus' name I declare this. Amen!"

EVENING ASSIGNMENT:

Before you sleep tonight, anoint your entire body with the oil and the communion. Declare the following. This is a very powerful prayer. Say it with authority:

"In the name of Jesus, I rebuke every spirit of lust. You will not attach yourself unto me! The Lord has delivered me. I release the blood of Jesus Christ in this house. I will sleep peacefully tonight. I will not be bombarded with sexual thoughts or have the desire to masturbate, in the name of Jesus. Lord Jesus, release Your angels in my home right now.

Send Your angels to fight every arrow released against me tonight, in the name of Jesus. Holy Spirit, dwell in my house. Holy Spirit, watch over me and give me sound sleep. I rebuke every agent of Satan released to rape me in my sleep and violate me sexually. I commend every incubus and succubus spirit to leave in the name of Jesus. Father, surround me with Your fire all night long. In Jesus' name, Amen."

CONFESSIONS TO CHRIST:

On the following blank page, to write in 5 sentences why soul ties are dangerous. *What are a few ways that they are formed?* Answer this question accord to what you have learned.

This concludes Day 17.

CONFESSIONS TO JESUS:

_____

_____

_____

_____

_____

_____

_____

_____

_____

_____

_____

_____

_____

_____

_____

_____

_____

_____

_____

_____

_____

_____

_____

_____

_____

_____

_____

_____

DAY 18: DON'T GO BACK TO EGYPT. BELIEVE IN YOUR DELIVERANCE.

MORNING:

Good morning, Overcomer! Take your communion. Before you pray this morning I want to share something with you.

It's somehow unbelievable that Israelites were tempted to return to Egypt—the land of bondage—even after witnessing the saving power of God **(Numbers 14:2-4)**. Of course, their exodus was quite challenging and they encountered many problems all along, they seemed oblivious of God's omnipotence and His willingness to deliver on His promises to them. In spite of Moses' leadership and his effort in reminding them of God's promise of security over their lives and possessions, they kept complaining about their ordeals. They put their mind off of God and wished they had been in Egypt, forgetting the cruelty of the Egyptians toward them while in the land. The people despised the Promise Land and provoked God.

Don't point an accusing finger at them yet. Do you know many Christians do the same thing, including yourself? We pray, asking God to deliver them from our trouble and after we have found freedom and respite, we relapse to the destructive behavior, lifestyle, or habit we wanted to escape in the first place. We live in a cycle of defeat. Most of us can relate to this in our personal lives behind closed doors.

I can remember those days of my struggle with masturbation. After a long struggle, I chose to align myself with God for absolute deliverance. Graciously, He revealed to me how I could use fasting to break free from the bondage each time I felt the tempting urge to indulge in the habit. The freedom began to increase, as I gained more ground spiritually, until one day when I began to fall into backsliding. Suddenly, the Spirit of God shouted at me in my spirit, "Don't go back to Egypt!" That voice was enough to help me snap back into consciousness so I could retrace my steps back to the Lord.

So I say to you too, DON'T GO BACK TO EGYPT! Don't go back to pornography, masturbation, and fornication.

SCRIPTURE:

Psalm 143:10 *"Teach me Your will for You are my God. May Your Gracious Spirit lead me forward on a firm footing."*

Say this prayer:

"Father God, in the name of Jesus. Lord help me not fall into temptation today. Lead me and order my steps. Teach me, Father, how to do Your will. Continue to give me the grace to pray and make fasting a lifestyle. Help me continue to grow strong in Your word. Help me continue to trust You even when all hell breaks loose! Help me trust You even when everything seems so impossible. Help me continue to listen to Your calm voice even when the enemy is shouting and lying! You have the last say. I love You and I thank You. In the name of Jesus, Amen!"

EVENING ASSIGNMENT:

Reflect on **Psalm 143:10** again. I believe the Lord released this word because you are afraid of backsliding or falling after this journey. But if you continue to ask HIM to teach you His will, you will never have the desire to fornicate. His Gracious Spirit will lead you forward and set your feet firmly in His word and in His path. You will not be lukewarm. You will not stumble and fall for another man that will just "hit it then quit it." Continue to dig deep in His word. Don't just read it; meditate on it and understand it.

Your assignment is to write in 5 sentences your understanding of the scripture above—**Psalm 143:10**.

CONFESSIONS TO CHRIST:

In the following blank page, write an 8 sentence letter to Jesus. Tell Him how you want Him to lead you after this journey is over. *What doubts and fears do you still have?* Start the letter with *"Dear Father, lead me ..."*

CONFESSIONS TO JESUS:

DAY 19: STICK TO THE VOW

MORNING:

Good morning, Overcomer! Take your communion and say this prayer:

"In the name of Jesus, I am no longer in Egypt! In the name of Jesus, I have been set free and delivered from EVERYTHING that causes me to fall short of the glory of God. In the name of Jesus, no voice from hell or whispering from Satan will deceive me. In the name of Jesus Christ, devil, you will not lie that I am not delivered. I am NO longer the same person that I was! I am not longer bound in chains. I am set free in Jesus' name. ALL the glory belongs to God for delivering me. This very moment, I refuse to listen to any voice that I contrary to the word of God. I rebuke everything that I hear to deceive me. The power of the word of God overcomes every demon, every lie, every deception and every fear in Jesus' name. Oh, by the blood of the lamb I am set free. My deliverance is permanent in Jesus' name. Amen!"

SCRIPTURE:

1 Corinthians 5:11 *"But now I am writing to you that you must not associate with anyone who claims to be a brother or sister but is sexually immoral or greedy, an idolater or slanderer, a drunkard or swindler. Do not even eat with such people."*

Ecclesiastes 5:4 *"When you make a vow to God, do not delay to fulfill it. He has no pleasure in fools; fulfill your vow."*

Be firm in His word and don't be a hypocrite! Don't be double-minded. Be set apart. There are so many free and affordable Christian events in every city. Do your research. But be open to the Spirit of the Lord and ask Him for discernment when you go to these Christian events or social gatherings because many "so-called" Christians are dressed in wolf's clothing. Yes, you can still have a great time, but be wise and discern.

EVENING ASSIGNMENT:

Perhaps you can relate to my past experience. The Lord has delivered you from an ungodly habit or relationship, and you feel yourself slipping back into your old ways. Let me be the one to tell you today that you are not at the mercy of your old habits of sexual activities. If you have received Christ as your Lord and Savior, then you are filled and equipped with the Spirit of the living God, and you can accomplish things in His strength and power that will amaze you. The Apostle Paul declared: *"I have strength for all things in Christ Who empowers me [I am ready for anything and equal to anything through Him Who infuses inner strength into me; I am self-sufficient in Christ's sufficiency]"* **(Philippians 4:13 AMP)**. Once you get a revelation of the Risen Christ living on the inside of you, God's strength will overcome your weaknesses. The best way to get this kind of revelation is to have your mind renewed by the Word of God. Study it, memorize it, meditate on it, and apply to every area of your life. Jesus said the truth would set us free **(John 8:36)** and that keeping our minds and hearts focused on the truth will bring the ultimate freedom. Then we've got to make up our minds to stand fast in that freedom, as the Bible instructs. *"It is for freedom that Christ has set us free. Stand firm, then, and do not let yourselves be burdened again by a yoke of slavery"* **(Galatians 5:1 NIV)**. Are you struggling with the temptation to backslide today? If you listen carefully, you just might hear the voice of God's precious Spirit pleading with you--"Don't go back to Egypt..."

Psalm 143:10 (NLT) *"Teach me to do Your will, for you are my God. May Your Gracious Spirit lead me forward on a firm footing."*

Anoint your entire body before you go to sleep tonight and make the declarations:

"In the name of Jesus, I am totally healed and restored from my past! I no longer have the lust of the flesh nor do I desire to fornicate! I hate sin; I rebuke it in the name of Jesus. My body is blessed. My body is anointed. My body is beautiful and only to be enjoyed by MY HUSBAND! I rebuke every incubus spirit in the name of JESUS. You will you NOT sexually violate me in my sleep nor will you torment me! I will not masturbate in the name of Jesus! I put on the full armor of God as I apply the anointing oil that breaks the yoke! I command angels from heaven to visit me in my sleep. Holy Spirit, give me visions; Holy Spirit, cause me to have divine dreams tonight! Father, in the name of Jesus, take full authority of my house tonight. Let Your consuming FIRE destroy every evil spirit and demonic visitation. "For we do not wrestle against flesh and blood, but against principalities, against powers, against the rulers of the darkness of this age, against spiritual hosts of wickedness in the heavenly places" (Ephesians 6:12). Therefore, Lord, guard me. Be my helper tonight. Be my warrior tonight as I sleep. In Jesus' name I pray, Amen."

After this prayer, get in the mood of worship. Go to YouTube and in the search type "Tye Tribbett feat. KJ Scrivens -What Can I Do with Lyrics."

CONFESSION TO CHRIST:

On the following blank page, write a 5-8 sentence letter to Jesus telling Him 3 things you want Him to do for you before the end of 2017. Start the letter with *"Dear Father, I am grateful that You have bought me this far, Lord I..."*

This ends Day 19.

CONFESSIONS TO JESUS:

DAY 20: LOOSING FRIENDS BUT GAINING CHRIST

MORNING:

Good morning, Overcomer! Take your communion and say this short prayer:

"Father, as I begin this day, let it be with You. Have Your way in everything that happens in my life today. I no longer want to make my own decisions without Your guidance. I no longer want to do things on my own without hearing from You. My desire is to hear from You every day. I no longer want my life wrapped up in distractions to only pull me away from Your will. As this journey comes to an end, bring Godly people in my life; bring God fearing men and women in my life. Align me with company and friends that practice Bible principles and fear You. Connect me with people that will help me grow spiritually. People that are genuinely in love with and do right by You. People that are thirsty for You and people that can help me whenever I am weak in this walk.

Father, release them now in the name of Jesus. Release them at my job, in my business, at church and wherever I go, even in the grocery store or at the gym. In the name of Jesus, I pray. Amen."

You are just a day from completing this journey and you should be very proud of yourself. It has not been easy. But as you can testify all things are possible with God, you cannot be stopped by the enemy himself. I also want to remind you that you are set apart and can no longer blend with fornicator and sinners.

SCRIPTURE:

1 Corinthians 5:11 *"But now I am writing to you that you must not associate with anyone who claims to be a brother or sister but is sexually immoral or greedy, an idolater or slanderer, a drunkard or swindler. Do not even eat with such people."*

Ecclesiastes 5:4 *"When you make a vow to God, do not delay to fulfill it. He has no pleasure in fools; fulfill your vow."*

EVENING ASSIGNMENT:

You are going to notice a difference in some friendships since rededicating your life fully to God. At times it will come in a form of mocking. This will also come in the form of rejection.

At first, this will be very hard to swallow and will feel as if you are being torn between two worlds. It was great getting invites to dinner or drinks with friends, and yet you now have so many exciting changes happening in your life that would want to share. It will seem clear that the topic is odd and perhaps a little unbelievable.

There will be days that you will feel like an outcast and when it happens; ask God to help you choose between faith and friends and pray for his continued guidance. He will give you revelation on spiritual suffering. Suffering for our faith comes with our continued growth.

When we draw closer to God, we can end up suffering on many levels—physically, mentally, emotionally and spiritually—but suffering in the name of Jesus is a high compliment. In fact, Scripture says, *"If you are insulted for the name of Christ, you are blessed, because the Spirit of glory and of God rests upon you"* **(1 Peter 4:14)**.

This isn't to say it feels good to lose friends or see some friendships weaken. It isn't to say that we should want or seek persecution or that it will even happen to us all. But it does test our character, endurance and sincere attempt to live by faith.

Evil will do all it can to work through situations and people to cause us to doubt or even abandon our paths. By understanding that we have to lose our life to gain it (even if that means a certain type of social life or "worldly" standard of living), we embrace the totality of the life God gave us to live, the one with doors waiting to open and miracles waiting to happen.

And losing friends doesn't mean forever. Differences challenge us, but the challenge is a good one. It's during the tough times that we discover what we're made of, especially when we endure them while remaining respectful and kind to others. (A sign of spiritual maturity!)

CONFESSIONS TO CHRIST:

On the following blank page, write the Lord a letter explaining to Him how you feel about losing certain relationships because you have decided to follow Him and His principles. Begin the letter with *"Dear Lord, I thank You for disconnecting me from ...."*

This ends Day 20.

CONFESSIONS TO JESUS:

_____
_____
_____
_____
_____
_____
_____
_____
_____
_____
_____
_____
_____
_____
_____
_____
_____
_____
_____
_____
_____
_____
_____
_____
_____
_____
_____

DAY 21: YOUR DELIVERANCE IS PERMANENT

MORNING:

Good morning, Overcomer! Take your communion and say this prayer:

"Lord Jesus You are truly amazing. Thank You for delivering me from fornication. Thank You for setting me free from pornography, thank You for delivering me from ungodly friends, thank You for delivering me from masturbation. Thank You that I am no longer the same person. Oh, in the name of Jesus. I commend every counter attack and retaliation because I have been obedient. Be destroyed in the name of Jesus. I will not black-slide, in the name of Jesus. Father let Your fire destroy every agent of Satan, the enemy, is preparing to distract me, even on this day in the name of Jesus. I am an overcomer. Fire of the Holy Spirit, consume every agenda of the enemy. Lord Jesus, cancel every assignment of Ishmael the enemy is preparing for me. Let every gate of hell be shut in my life in Jesus' name. Every evil pit of sexual immorality prepared for me be destroyed right now by the blood of Jesus. I will continue to be celibate until marriage in

the name of Jesus. This body belongs to Jesus and for sexual purposes it was only meant for my husband, in Jesus' name. I bind and rebuke any man with evil intentions to only sleep with me and abuse me in Jesus' name. I am healed from every rape and sexual abuse in the name of Jesus. Father, give me discernment, in the name of Jesus! Open my spiritual eyes to see between the wolf and the sheep in Jesus' name. Lord Jesus, continue to grace me with strength to continue on the journey of celibacy until marriage. I thank You and I Love You, In Jesus' name Amen!"

You will never be the same woman that you were 21 days ago. The Lord has done a great work in you. Your mind, body, soul and spirit are renewed. The Lord has delivered you in 21 days from a stronghold and battle you have been struggling with for years! Go to church this morning and spend time in the house of The Lord.

SCRIPTURE:

Luke 4:18 *"The Spirit of the Lord is upon me, because he hath anointed me to preach the gospel to the poor; he hath sent me to heal the brokenhearted, to preach deliverance to the captives, recover sight to the blind, and to set at liberty them that are bruised."*

EVENING:

You can now share the good news with others. You are now a testament of what God can do in the life of a fornicator. You now have the passion to help someone that is battling with this sin and you have the responsibility to tell them about the healing grace of Jesus and the power of His deliverance.

Isaiah 43:19 *"See, I am doing a new thing! Now it springs up; do you not perceive it? I am making a way in the wilderness and streams in the wasteland."*

Before you sleep tonight, take a bath or shower. Anoint your entire body with the anointing oil and repeat the same prayer you declared this morning.

CONFESSIONS TO CHRIST:

On the following page, write a 10 sentence letter to Jesus and reflect on these last 21 days. Say whatever comes to mind. Speak to Him from your heart.

This completes the journey. Congratulations!

CONFESSIONS TO JESUS:

_____
_____
_____
_____
_____
_____
_____
_____
_____
_____
_____
_____
_____
_____
_____
_____
_____
_____
_____
_____
_____
_____
_____
_____
_____

STEPS TO MAINTAINING YOUR DELIVERANCE

If you're serious about getting delivered, you need to know and appropriate certain principles (in addition to those required to break soul ties). The following steps will work effectively now that you have broken any previous soul tie and repented of your involvement in any other form of sexual sin. Demons often hide behind unconfessed sins and unbroken soul ties to lay hold on their victims.

As we go, rest assured that God has set you free whether the incubus/succubus spirit is no longer inside of you—in your body—or attacking you from without. In other words, demons work in two ways; they may be living inside the body of their host or be occasionally coming from somewhere to attack the person. You have been delivered and set free. You have to continue to pray, fast, and live a consecrated life to maintain your deliverance.

Renounce the incubus/succubus spirit that has infiltrated your body—your life—and renounce their activities. Also, verbally renounce every element (e.g. fear, lethargy, weakness) they have deposited into you. Command such things to vanish in the name of Jesus. Such things are their offspring. You need to deal with both the spirit and their offspring for your total liberation.

1. **Continue to commend to them to go out in the name of Jesus.** Then command those ones that are without to stop coming to you.

2. **After this, if you still have sexual dreams, rise up and abort what they have deposited in you.** They are only trying to regain their original place in you. So don't give them a foothold. Before you sleep each night, cover your whole mind—the subconscious and the unconscious—with the blood of the Lamb and ask God to awake you whenever you start having a sex dream.

3. **See your deliverance as a battle.** Always challenge the spirits each time they come to oppress you, no matter how terrible the nightmare you might have. Never entertain fear; they want you to believe that you're not making any progress. Challenge them but if you're still living a sinful lifestyle, you would play a host to them— they won't leave.

4. **Whenever you have an unusual sexual urge to watch porn or commit fornication and masturbation, speak over your body.** *"You spirit of sexual lust, I rebuke and resist you in Jesus' name! My body is the temple of the Holy Spirit, so it doesn't belong to you. Go away in Jesus' name! I reject the seed you're trying to deposit into me!"* Afterwards, get yourself engaged with a spiritually edifying activity like writing, listening to gospel music, or watching a preacher on TV; and fill your mind with good thoughts.

5. **Gather and throw away all items relating to sex, such as movie DVDs, novels, magazines, and romantic music CDs.** They serve as doorways to evil spirits. You won't be delivered if you still hold onto these things. In addition, keep off things like Internet pornography, soap operas, horror movies, etc.

6. **When sharing your experience with someone, maybe a counselor or your pastor, don't describe it in a graphic way.** Doing such will give life to the seed or offspring of the spirits. Just tell that you had a sex dream—that's all. In the same vein, when you awake from a sex dream, never try to recall the scenes in your mind. Give your mind to something productive and edifying and cast it out in the name of Jesus.

7. **Now that you have repented of your sins, rededicate your whole being to the Lord Jesus Christ.** Ask the Holy Spirit to fill you and close every door against the demons. On your part, as noted earlier, don't have anything to do with things, people, or places that can grant access to sex demons. Whatever weaknesses you allow in your life will invite these spirits back. Begin to seek the Kingdom of God and His righteousness from now **(Matthew 6:33)**.

8. **Give yourself to prayer and fasting.** Fasting is often necessary to your deliverance, considering the fact that demons are stubborn spirits that don't want to be evicted from their place of rest. Use prayer and fasting to rout them.

9. **Read good Christian and motivational books that will help you understand all you need to know about sex and related topics.** Read books that will enhance your relationship with the Lord. This is very important.

LAST WORDS

All of us might not have become a victim of the spirit of fornication. But then, there are other manifestations, as the spirit of lust daily attempts to lure us into sin through our mind. These spirits know that you don't have to be physically engaged in the act to commit the sin; you only need to look and lust after a person to be found guilty.

Today, lust is everywhere—on the street, the media, the internet, etc. Every day, you come across lust, maybe in the form of half-naked ladies in your workplace. *What would you do?* The answer has to do with your mind. The mind is the battleground. We are all surrounded by temptations of lust, which is a prime tool of Satan in the 21st century. You will face the temptation, but don't fall into it.

With the power of attorney from God, you can use the name of Jesus to deal with those demons and they will obey you. After having done all, after having been delivered, stand firm in the liberty you have received, so that you won't be entangled again with the yoke of bondage **(Galatians 5:1)**. Amen.

ABOUT THE AUTHOR

A true lover of Jesus Christ, Linda Chiyoge, radiates with the love and the joy of the Lord. Linda transcended barriers and defeated odds. Her incredible story is one that leaves "no excuses" to anyone that wants to better their lives; by allowing Jesus Christ to be the center of their obstacles, pain, and failures. Before becoming an over-comer, she faced an extreme abusive marriage, traumatic divorce followed by a devastating cycle of heartbreaks and disappointments from multiple relationships that resulted in public shame and defamation of character. She eventually found her inner strength by the help of Jesus through fasting, prayer, and deliverance. She has taken control over her sorrowful past and used it as the foundation to fulfill her purpose.

She has influenced thousands of women through social media by sharing her remarkable testimony and teaching them bible principles and giving them spiritual tools to overcome obstacles that they face when it comes to issues of the heart.

Besides manifesting in her God-ordained assignment of loving people and being used by God to mend broken hearts, she's also a strong advocate of practicing purity, holiness and truly honoring The Lord with our body as living sacrifice and refraining from sexual immorality. She has been abstinence for almost 6 years and she encourages and leads unmarried women to do the same through her programs.

Linda's transparency and rawness of her testimony have gained her prominence among her peers. Linda believes everyone possesses purpose and passion.

She is passionate about helping women escape unhealthy and abusive relationships. Her main goal is to help women see themselves as God sees them and recognize that we've been created with and for a purpose. Helping women understand their worth and position in the Kingdom is her true calling!

She is clothed with strength and dignity; she can laugh at the days to come.

-Proverbs 31:25

43978946R00113

Made in the USA
Middletown, DE
01 May 2019